The Book of Numbers

The Book of Numbers

A Study Manual

by

Kenneth E. Jones

BAKER BOOK HOUSE
Grand Rapids, Michigan

ISBN: O-8010-5010-3

Copyright, 1972, by

Baker Book House Company

PRINTED IN THE UNITED STATES OF AMERICA

CONTENTS

Introduction 7

Outline and Analysis 13

I.   Encampment at Sinai (1:1–10:10) 17

II.   Sinai to Paran (10:11–12:16) 35

III. In Paran (13:1–19:22) 45

IV.   March from Kadesh to Moab (20:1–22:1) 59

V.   The Story of Balaam (22:2–24:25) 68

VI.   Miscellaneous Laws and Incidents (25:1–32:42) 76

VII. Recapitulation and Appendixes (33:1–36:13) 86

INTRODUCTION

Name. Numbers, in the Hebrew Bible, is called *Bemidbar,* "In the Wilderness." This is the fourth word in the first chapter, and is a good description of the contents of the book, since it tells of events on the way from Egypt to Canaan. The English title comes from the fact that in the book there are reports of two censuses of the people of God, in Chapters 1 and 26. In the German Bible, it is known as the Fourth Book of Moses.

Contents. This book begins at Mount Sinai and ends with the people of God encamped on the northern boundary of Moab at the Jordan River, making plans to cross over into the promised land. It takes up the story of the travels through the wilderness at about the time the Book of Exodus ends, or one month before.

In contrast to the Book of Leviticus, which is mostly law, Numbers combines history and law. So there is far more interest and value in the book than the name in English would imply. Only two chapters are census reports (1 and 26). The rest tells of events between Sinai and the Jordan. For the most part these are not recorded elsewhere except for the brief summary in the first chapters of Deuteronomy. Interspersed with this history are religious and civil laws and instructions. Many of these are presented as preparation for settling in the land of Canaan, and it is expressly stated that they are for that time, rather than for the time at which they were given.

The events recorded in this book center around three locations: Sinai, Kadesh-Barnea, and Moab. These three places form the basis for a rough division of the book into three parts: Sinai (1-10), Kadesh (11-21), Moab (22-36). A more detailed outline of the book is difficult to make because of the miscellaneous character of Numbers. In some instances it is difficult to see what is the pattern of arrangement of material. Yet this comes from the mixed nature of the material itself, which is both narrative and law. The narrative moves forward chronologically, but the law is put into the midst of the narrative wherever it is directly or indirectly relevant to something in the narrative, or because it was given to the people at that point in their travels.

The events of the Book of Numbers cover forty years. Thirty-eight years of this time are passed over in almost complete silence, so that basically the book is concerned with the first few months and the last year or so of these forty years of wandering in the wilderness. Only two events are described out of these long years of punishment for their reaction to the report of the spies sent from Kadesh. Those two events are the revolt of Korah and other Levites and Reubenites (chap. 16), and the budding of Aaron's rod (chap. 17). So the Bible tells about this period of punishment for lack of faith, but refuses to dwell on it.

Moses, Aaron, and Miriam are the leading persons of this story, but there is no question that Moses is the leading character. The death of both Aaron and Miriam is recorded here, and the death of Moses is predicted. None of the three was permitted to live to see the entrance into Canaan.

Author. Moses is clearly the outstanding person in the Book of Numbers, and has traditionally been considered its author, though very early Ezra was suggested as an alternate possibility. The book itself, except for Chapter 33, does not claim to have been written by Moses. It does, however, claim throughout to report speeches of Moses, and messages given to Moses by God. So while Numbers does not claim Mosaic authorship, in the modern sense that Moses wrote down every word, it does emphatically claim Mosaic and divine authority.

Numbers makes strong claim to divine authority. More than eighty times it is said that *God spoke to Moses,* and more than one hundred times it is said that *God spoke.* Yet the book does not hesitate to quote from an older book of which we have no knowledge (Num. 21:14). The divine authority which is claimed throughout is not dependent on Mosaic authorship, as such, since God could as easily have guided other persons in the writing.

Mosaic authority for this book does not necessarily imply that every word was written down by Moses. He had a good education, and was perfectly capable of writing this record. We do not have to believe that he did so. A few things in the book seem clearly to have been added after the time of Moses (e.g., 15:22 ff.).

The nineteenth century theory of tracing the origin of the first five books of the Bible, including Numbers, to documents which were written at various times and compiled not long before Christ, has been strongly modified. When recent scholars speak of J E D P, they do not mean documents, but something like strands of tradition. They also do not think so much of a rigid time schedule by which these "documents" were written, as of a long process of development which culminated in the books in their present form. According to this view, most of the material in the Book of Numbers is considered to be from the P (priestly) source. In the last century, the view has been common that such material was written after the Exile, and perhaps after Ezra. The latter would be nearly a thousand years after Moses. But there is a growing tendency to agree that there is very early material represented in P. Conservative scholars in general insist on the Mosaic origin of the whole book.

Value. The misleading name given to this book in our English Bibles has kept many from being aware of the great values in it for Christians. First, we have the record of the way God led the people from Sinai to the Jordan River. It is true that this record is briefly summarized in the first three chapters of Deuteronomy, but many of the interesting details are omitted there. The emphasis in Numbers is not in listing the events, but in giving their spiritual meaning. Here we see not merely a group of people struggling toward independence, but God working with them to bring them to the point where He wants them to be.

Second, we have some laws in this book which are not given in the rest of the Old Testament, or not explained so fully. For example, in Chapters 28-29 we have a list of the feast days of the year, and their dates according to the Jewish calendar. Some of the sacrifices are described only here, or only here in such detail. This book describes in some instances the situation in which certain laws were applied. That is helpful in understanding their relevance. If it were not for Numbers 19, we would not know the background of Hebrews 13:11-12.

Third, the book is full of spiritual lessons for the Christian who learns to see them. The Book of Hebrews, to some extent, points the way. For example, Hebrews 3:7 ff. points out a great application of Numbers 13-14 to the Christian life. And Jesus used 21:5-9 as an illustration of what He was trying to say about His own death and His offer of salvation to all (John 3:14 ff.).

For Further Study:

Brief, but helpful:

Oswald T. Allis. *God Spake by Moses.* Philadelphia: Presbyterian and Reformed Publishing Co., 1951.

A. A. MacRae. "Numbers" in *The New Bible Commentary.* Grand Rapids: Eerdmans, 1954.

More exhaustive treatments:

George Buchanan Gray, *Numbers* ("International Critical Commentary"). New York: Scribners, 1906.

Howard A. Hanke. "Numbers" in *The Wesleyan Bible Commentary,* Vol. One, Part 1. Grand Rapids: Eerdmans, 1967.

J. H. Hertz. "Numbers" in *The Pentateuch and Haftorahs.* New York: Soncino Press, 1960.

J. Du Bois Lauriston. "Numbers" in *Beacon Bible Commentary,* Vol. 1. Kansas City: Beacon Hill Press, 1967.

A. H. McNeile. *The Book of Numbers* (Cambridge Bible for Schools and Colleges). New York: Cambridge University Press, 1931.

Martin Noth. *Numbers, A Commentary.* Philadelphia: The Westminster Press, 1968.

OUTLINE AND ANALYSIS

I. ENCAMPMENT AT SINAI (1:1–10:10)
    A. Census of Tribes and Duties of Levites (1:1-54)
        1. Appointment of Census Takers (1:1-19)
        2. Numbers of the Tribes (1:20-46)
        3. Duties of the Levites (1:47-54)
    B. Position of the Tribes on the March and in Camp (2:1-34)
    C. Special Position of the Levites (3:1-51)
        1. Sons of Aaron (3:1-4)
        2. Duties of the Levites (3:5-10)
        3. Significance of the Levites (3:11-13)
        4. Levitical Census, Positions, and Duties (3:14-39)
        5. Numbering of Israel's First-born (3:40-51)
    D. Numbers and Duties of the Levites (4:1-49)
        1. The Kohathites (4:1-20)
        2. The Gershonites (4:21-28)
        3. The Merarites (4:29-33)
        4. Census of the Levites (4:34-49)
    E. Miscellaneous Laws and Regulations (5:1–6:27)
        1. Isolation of the Unclean (5:1-4)
        2. Restitution of Stolen Property (5:5-10)
        3. Ordeal of Jealousy (5:11-31)
        4. Regulations for the Nazirities (6:1-21)
        5. The Priestly Blessing (6:22-27)
    F. The Princes' Offerings (7:1-88)
    G. Miscellaneous Laws (7:89–10:10)
        1. The Golden Lampstand (8:1-4)
        2. Purification and Presentation of the Levites (8:5-22)
        3. Age Limits for Levites (8:23-26)
        4. The Supplementary Passover (9:1-14)
        5. The Fiery Cloud (9:15-23)
        6. The Silver Trumpets (10:1-10)

II. SINAI TO PARAN (10:11–12:16)
    A. Departure from Sinai (10:11-36)
        1. Time and Order of Departure (10:11-28)
        2. Moses' Father-in-law (10:29-32)
        3. Movements of the Ark (10:33-36)
    B. Various incidents (11:1-35)

       1. Complaints at Taberah (11:1-3)
       2. Complaints about Manna (11:4-10)
       3. Moses' Expostulation with Yahweh (11:11-15)
       4. Yahweh's Reply to Moses (11:16-24a)
       5. Eldership and Prophecy (11:24b-30)
       6. The Supply of Meat (11:31-35)
   C. Miriam, Aaron, and Moses (12:1-16)
       1. Complaint against Moses (12:1-2)
       2. The Meekness of Moses (12:3)
       3. Moses' Vindication (12:4-10)
       4. Moses' Intercession for Miriam (12:11-16)

III. IN PARAN (13:1–19:22)
   A. The Spies (13:1–14:45)
       1. Appointment of Twelve Spies (13:1-17a)
       2. Briefing of the Spies (13:17b-20)
       3. The Territory Surveyed (13:21-24)
       4. The Spies' Return to Paran (13:25-26a)
       5. The Spies' Report (13:26b-33)
       6. Israel's Complaints (14:1-2)
       7. Design for Retreat (14:3-4)
       8. Report of Caleb and Joshua (14:5-9)
       9. Tragedy Averted (14:10)
     10. God's Threat and Moses' Intercession (14:11-25)
     11. Yahweh's Punishment Pronounced (14:26-38)
     12. Attempted Invasion Defeated (14:39-45)
   B. Miscellaneous Laws (15:1-41)
       1. Flour, Oil, and Wine for Sacrifice (15:1-16)
       2. Offerings of Coarse Meal (15:17-21)
       3. Offerings for Unknown Sins (15:22-29
       4. Punishment for Defiant Sinners (15:30, 31)
       5. A Sabbath Breaker's Fate (15:32-36)
       6. Wearing Tassels (15:37-41)
   C. Rebellion of Korah, Dathan, and Abiram (16:1–17:13)
       1. The Rebels (16:1-2)
       2. Korah's Rebellion (16:3-11)
       3. Revolt of Dathan and Abiram (16:12-15)
       4. Ordeal of Korah (16:16-24)
       5. Ordeal of Dathan and Abiram (16:25-34)
       6. Further Punishment (16:35-50)
       7. Sprouting of Aaron's Rod (17:1-13)
   D. Dues and Duties of Priests and Levites (18:1-32)
       1. Levites' Duties (18:1-7)
       2. Priests' Dues (18:8-20)

3. Levites' Dues (18:21-24)
4. Priests' Dues from the Levites (18:25-32)
E. Purification from Uncleanness by the Dead (19:1-22)
1. Rite of the Red Heifer (19:1-10)
2. General Procedure for Cleansing (19:11-13)
3. Specific Rules of Cleansing (19:14-22)

IV. MARCH FROM KADESH TO MOAB (20:1—22:1)
A. Sojourn at Kadesh (20:1-21)
1. Miriam's Death (20:1)
2. Miracle of Meribah (20:2-13)
3. Israel and Edom (20:14-21)
B. En route for Moab (20:22—22:1)
1. Aaron's Death (20:22-29)
2. Defeat and Victory at Hormah (21:1-3)
3. The Bronze Serpent (21:4-9)
4. On the March (21:10-20)
5. Defeat of the Amorites (21:21-32)
6. Defeat of Og (21:33-35)
7. Encampment Opposite Jericho (22:1)

V. THE STORY OF BALAAM (22:2—24:25)
A. Balak and Balaam (22:2-40)
1. Moab's Fear of Israel (22:2-4)
2. Balak's First Embassy (22:5-14)
3. Balak's Second Embassy (22:15-21)
4. Balaam and His Ass (22:22-35)
5. Balaam's Visit to Balak (22:36-40)
B. Balaam's Oracles (22:41—24:25)
1. First Oracle (22:41—23:12)
2. Second Oracle (23:13-26)
3. Third Oracle (23:27—24:13)
4. Farewell Oracle (24:14-25)

VI. MISCELLANEOUS LAWS AND INCIDENTS
(25:1—32:42)
A. Physical and Spiritual Wantonness (25:1-18)
1. Wantonness with Moab (25:1-5)
2. Wantonness with Midian (25:6-18)
B. Second Census (26:1-65)
C. Law of Female Inheritance (27:1-11)
D. Appointment of Joshua (27:12-23)
E. Laws of Public Worship (28:1—29:40)

F. The Law on Women's Vows (30:1-16)
G. Extermination of the Midianites (31:1-54)
   1. The Expeditionary Force (31:1-6)
   2. Defeat and Destruction of Midian (31:7-12)
   3. Order to Exterminate Midian (31:13-18)
   4. Warriors' Purification (31:19-24)
   5. Division of the Spoil (31:25-54)
H. Settlements in Trans-Jordan (32:1-42)
   1. Request of Gad and Reuben (32:1-5)
   2. Anger of Moses (32:6-15)
   3. Gad's and Reuben's Promises (32:16-19)
   4. Moses' Permission (32:20-33)
   5. Cities Built by Gad and Reuben (32:34-38)
   6. Manassite Settlements in Gilead (32:39-42)

VII. RECAPITULATION AND APPENDIXES (33:1—36:13)
A. Israel's Route from Egypt to Canaan (33:1-49)
B. Israel's Duty in Canaan (33:50-56)
C. Tribal Boundaries in Canaan (34:1-29)
   1. Boundaries Fixed (34:1-15)
   2. Allotment Officers (34:16-29)
D. Levitical Cities (35:1-34)
   1. Cities for the Levites (35:1-8)
   2. Cities of Refuge (35:9-15)
   3. Manslaughter and Murder (35:16-25)
   4. Legal Procedure and Warning (35:26-34)
E. Marriage of Heiresses (36:1-13)

I. ENCAMPMENT AT SINAI (1:1—10:10)

This whole section is a continuation of the story of Exodus. The people are still encamped at Mount Sinai, as at the end of that book. The Law had been given (Exod. 20), the covenant had been ratified (Exod. 21-24), the Tabernacle had been built and dedicated (Exod. 40), and the priestly services inaugurated (Lev. 9). Now this first section of Numbers tells of some of the further preparations for becoming a real people — the people of God. These include the counting and arrangement of the tribes, instructions about the Levites, and the celebration of the first Passover.

A. Census of Tribes and Duties of Levites (1:1-54)

This command of the Lord came while the newly freed slaves of the Egyptians were still at the foot of Mount Sinai, and just one month after the completion of the Tabernacle (Exod. 40:1-33). Stressing the importance of the command to take the census, we are told just when it came to Moses, and where he was at the time. He was in the Tent of Meeting, that is, the Tabernacle, or Tent of Revelation (cf. Exod. 39:12), since that was the regular place where God met with His spokesman.

The census described here is probably the same as that mentioned in Exodus 30:11 ff. and 38:25. There we are told that it was taken at the same time that a poll tax was collected for the building of the Tabernacle. The date mentioned here in Numbers is a few months later than the other, and indicates that this is the date of the completion of the census which was begun at the earlier date. This was a military census of the men eligible for military service, and was preparatory for the organization of the whole people as a nation.

1. Appointment of Census Takers (1:1-19). This census was not a count of all the people who had left Egypt, but of those men who were able to serve in the army (v. 3). It was no doubt an important factor in their development of a concept of nationhood.

God had led His covenant people out of Egypt for this, that they might become a nation, an independent and established people out of which would one day come the Messiah. But there was much to be done if this crowd of people were to achieve this exalted purpose of being a nation which would bless the nations. Certain vital steps had already been taken: God had given them Moses as their leader. He had given them a set of laws by which to be governed. He had given them a place and form of worship, with the priesthood. All of these served to bring the people together and give them a common center around which to rally. Now God was teaching them to organize themselves so that they would go on their way in orderly fashion, not as a mob.

It is stated that *the Lord spake unto Moses*, telling him how to carry out the census. This is the first of about eighty-five times in the Book of Numbers that it is specifically said that God spoke to Moses. So there is a strong emphasis in the whole book on the divine guidance of Moses as he led the people. There is the settled conviction that not only the worship of the people is directed by the will of God, but the whole of their social and national life. This is an important aspect of ancient Hebrew religion.

God directed the whole procedure to be carried out in a systematic manner. Moses and Aaron were told to arrange the people in tribes, clans, and families. From each of the twelve tribes was chosen a leader who was directly in charge of the count of that tribe, and who was responsible to Moses. The fact that these are then named presents a picture of an orderly procedure and an organized camp.

2. Numbers of the Tribes (1:20-46). The number of draft-age men in each tribe is now given in a list, and the total is given as 603,550. Many commentators feel that there is some problem with these figures, for they would imply a total population of at least two million. The problem becomes clear when we realize that this is the equivalent of a city larger than Washington, D.C.; consider how much water, food, and space is needed for that many people — and their flocks!

Some simply refuse to take the figures seriously, and suggest that they are either pure speculation, or constructed on some forgotten artificial scheme. Petrie suggested that perhaps the word *'eleph*, which is translated "thousand," really meant "family" or "clan." But Martin Noth has worked out what is probably the most plausible solution, and one which takes seriously the text of Numbers. Briefly, he suggests that the Hebrew word *'eleph* in the time of Moses meant "troop" but later came to be used for "thousand." This would be a very natural and expected linguistic change. He further suggests that centuries later the original meaning of the word had been forgotten, just as the original meaning of many English words are now completely unknown. So it was that later scribes misinterpreted the ancient figures and added up the figures as though the word meant "thousand." On this interpretation, the original figures would show that in the total of twelve tribes there were 598 troops of men, with a total of 5,550 soldiers. This would imply a total of fifteen or twenty thousand persons. Such a solution may or may not be correct, but is far better than a complete disregard of the Biblical record.

3. Duties of the Levites (1:47-54). God had a special purpose and work for the tribe of Levi, for which they were to be set apart and dedicated. For this reason, they were not to be counted among those who were able to go to war. The Levites, as is explained later, camped around the Tabernacle for its protection, instead of being gathered together on some one side, as was each of the other tribes. For the same reason, when the people entered into Canaan, the Levites were not assigned land for inheritance, as were the other tribes, but were supported by special donations from all the other tribes.

Verses 50-51 list some of the duties of the Levites. They were to be responsible for the Tabernacle and all the furnishings and cookware belonging to it. This was no small task, especially when the people were moving from one place to another. They were to do all the work connected with the Tabernacle and its use. And they were to see that everything about it was kept in usable condition and in its proper place, so that it could be found quickly when needed. Considerable organization and division of responsibilities was necessary if the Levites were to carry out their assignment.

Furthermore, only the Levites were to work in and around the Tabernacle (v. 51b). Anyone else who tried to help was to be put to death. This emphasized the need for care in the worship of God.

B. Position of the Tribes on the March and in Camp (2:1-34)

The emphasis of this chapter is on order and discipline. The people of Israel are not to be a disorganized mob, but a disciplined people — the people of God. Note how carefully plans are made for the people to camp and march in orderly fashion. Nothing is left to chance. God is teaching the people that just as He does all things systematically and carefully, so they must be orderly if they are to be His people.

As shown in the chart, the camp was organized in such a fashion that the Tabernacle itself was in the very center. Three tribes camped on each of the four sides, with Judah and the associated tribes of Zebulun and Issachar occupying the place of honor on the east side, in front of the Tabernacle. The four groups of Levites (Sons of Aaron, Merarites, Kohathites, and Gershonites) camped in a protective way between the Tabernacle and the other tribes.

The fact that the Tabernacle was in the center of the camp had a spiritual significance also. For the Tabernacle signified the presence of God. It was not the place where God was thought to live, but it symbolized His presence. God could not live in a physical structure (I Kings 8:27), though it is impossible for us to know how clearly the Hebrews at Sinai understood this. However, we do know that the Tabernacle differed from all other temples of that age in that there was in it no representation of God, or Yahweh! The Hebrews were absolutely forbidden to make any such images (Exod. 20:4-5; Deut. 5:8-11). In this, their religion was unique in the ancient world, as all of the nations around them made images of their gods, and believed that their gods dwelt in places, and often in temples. But even in the time of Moses, the Hebrews had a sure glimpse of the fact that Yahweh could not live in a tent or a building. So when they prepared to build the Tabernacle, they did not plan to build a place where God would live, but rather a place which would symbolize the presence of God in their midst, and a place in which they could meet with God in worship and prayer. Hence they called it a "tent of meeting" (v. 2 RSV). By this they did not mean that it was a place where the congregation met together, but where persons could meet with God. They were told to build the Tabernacle so that God might "dwell among them" (Exod. 25:8 KJV).

This means that even the arrangement of the camp was a part of the divine instruction. God was teaching the people to think of God as being always in their midst. God must be central in all that they did. Israel was a special people, with God in their midst.

C. Special Position of the Levites (3:1-51)

As was noted in the discussion of 1:47, the Levites were not included in the census of the rest of the tribes. They were honored by being counted in a separate census which is recorded in Chapter 4. Before that count is recorded, we are told of the special position of the Levites among the people of God.

1. Sons of Aaron (3:1-4). These verses are a repetition of Exodus 6:23 and Leviticus 10:1-2 in order to introduce this fuller explanation of the events; they also illustrate the significance of the Levites. In spite of the apparent meaning of verse 1, we do not have any record of descendants of Moses, and the chapter is about Moses appointing priests and Levites to their duties. (The Hebrew word *toledoth*, translated "generations," must here mean "events.")

Verse 4 is a summary of what is described in Leviticus 10:1-6, and vividly illustrates the rigidness with which the rules of worship were to be kept. None but Levites must serve in the sanctuary, and they must be careful to do everything according to instructions! The expression *unholy fire* could mean that common fire was used rather than fire from the altar (cf. Lev. 16:12); but the Hebrew expression is broad enough to cover any infringement of the rules of sacrifice. The point being emphasized is that the Levites, and the Levites alone, are to serve in the Tabernacle, and they must be careful to do it properly.

2. Duties of the Levites (3:5-10). The fact that the whole tribe of Levites were to be set apart for the work of the Tabernacle was both a great privilege and a great responsibility for them, and one in which they had no individual choice. If they were born into this tribe, then this was the work they had to share.

The whole tribe was under the general direction of Aaron, who is here described as *priest*, but who was really the "high priest" (see Exod. 28). The Levites were special servants of Aaron (v. 6) and representatives of the whole nation in the service of the Tabernacle (v. 7). The common people were not allowed to serve in the sanctuary, so the Levites were their agents in this service. This is what is meant by keeping the *charge of the whole congregation* (v. 7).

The *furnishings* (v. 8) included, besides the furniture of the Tabernacle, all the vessels, pots, tongs, and such things, which were used in the work of offering various kinds of sacrifices. All of the many kinds of things which were used in the work of sacrifices and ceremonies were to be cared for by the Levites alone. Since these things were to be used in the worship of God, there were strict rules as to their care and use. None of them could ever be used in secular work, or for any purposes other than those for which they were specifically made. It was the task of the Levites to use them properly, so as not to defile them.

Note that the Levites are to be *wholly given* to Aaron and his sons — the priests. The statement (v. 9) represents a very strong form of repetition of verbs in the Hebrew. This expresses the life-long dedication which God demanded of the Levites. They must give their whole lives to the service of Aaron in the work of the Tabernacle. These duties are outlined as they were necessary during the travels in the wilderness, even though they changed somewhat after the conquest of Canaan and the establishment of a settled place of worship.

So the Levites alone are permitted to do the work of the Tabernacle. If others came near, they were to be executed (v. 10). One purpose of such restriction was to teach the meaning of *sacredness* and *holiness*. Things dedicated to God must not be used for ordinary purposes or in ordinary ways. Persons dedicated to God are separated from ordinary duties and ways.

3. Significance of the Levites (3:11-13). In relation of Aaron and Moses, the Levites are to be regarded as the spiritual family (vv. 3-4) with Aaron as the head of the family. But in relation to the rest of the tribes, the Levites are specially consecrated to God *instead of every firstborn son* (v. 12). They thus represent the firstborn sons of all the tribes. This fact is the basis on which the Levites shared in the produce and goods of all the tribes, as first-born sons would do.

Verse 13 reminds us of the historical reason for the importance of the firstborn. From the time of the slaying of the firstborn in Egypt (both of the Egyptians and of the apostate Israelites), the firstborn son was dedicated to God and given certain priestly functions. At the time of the worship of the Golden Calf (Exod. 32), the Levites proved themselves worthy of honor and special responsibilities. So God chose them to serve in the place of the firstborn sons of all the tribes (Num. 3:40 ff), and the firstborn of all the tribes were released from their privileges and responsibilities.

4. Levitical Census, Positions, and Duties (3:14-39). As we have seen, the Levites were not included in the first census of the tribes. Some features of their special census are different from the general one. The primary difference is that the rest of the people were counted from the age of twenty years, and the Levites from the age of one month. The reason is that the Levites

were substitutes for the firstborn, and that one month is the age at which the firstborn could be redeemed, or substituted for (Num. 18:16).

Each tribe was made up of clans, and each clan consisted of families. At least, these would be our usual designations, though the Hebrew word usually translated "family" means something closer to "clan." Verses 14-20 give the names of the heads of the clans or families of the Levite tribe. The three clans were the descendants of Gershon, Kohath, and Merari.

In verses 21-37 we are told of the numbers of each of the three clans or divisions of Levites, where each was to camp, and what their duties were. The Gershonites (7,500) were to camp behind the Tabernacle, on the west, and have the general care of the outside of it. The Kohathites (8,600) camped on the south, and had charge of the sacred vessels used in the Tabernacle. The Merarites (6,200) camped on the north, and were responsible for the boards, pillars and sockets. In each case, the Levites camped between the Tabernacle and the other tribes.

This means that the Levites were divided into their three divisions and camped on three sides of the Tabernacle. In front of the Tabernacle, on the east, Moses himself and the Aaronic priests were to camp, since they were to conduct the actual ceremonies in the sanctuary (v. 38).

There is an obvious error in copying in verse 39, where the total number of Levites is given as 22,000, since simple addition of the figures given (7500, 8600, and 6200) shows the total as 22,300. Certain numbers look so much alike in Hebrew that it is easy to understand how such an error could occur.

5. Numbering of Israel's First-born (3:40-51). As shown in verse 13, all the firstborn belong to the Lord. But since the Levites were now dedicated to the service of the Lord in relation to the Tabernacle, they *redeem* the firstborn; that is, they liberate the firstborn from their special relationship and responsibility. One Levite is accepted for one of the firstborn. Since there were 273 more firstborn than Levites, money was given for this number (vv. 46-47). This was in accord with the law in Leviticus 27. This money was given to Aaron and his sons (v. 51).

D. Numbers and Duties of the Levites (4:1-49)

A second census of the Levites is recorded in this chapter, but this one is only of those Levites between the ages of thirty and fifty (vv. 3, 23, 30), which is the twenty-year period during which each of them served the Tabernacle. The chief purpose of this chapter is to spell out the duties of the various clans in more detail.

1. The Kohathites (4:1-20). Kohath was the second son of Levi, but is listed first here since the sons of Kohath had the more important duties.

Note that the three divisions or clans of Levites are discussed in three closely parallel passages. Notice the repetition of stereotyped phrases. This is rather common in several parts of the Old Testament. It is especially fitting in presenting this sort of census material, which necessitates some repetition. In each of these three sections, the command is first given for the census of the division (vv. 2, 22, 29), and the age limits are given (vv. 3, 23, 30). Then the specific duties of the division are described. Each section ends with the same sentence, and the naming of the person to be general supervisor of the work of that division (vv. 15c-16, 28, 33).

The Kohathites, under the supervision of Eleazer, the priest, were to have charge of the Ark, the table, the candlestick, the altars, the veil, and the vessels used in the Tabernacle. They were to carry them when the Israelites moved, but they were to be careful not to touch them. The priests would carefully wrap each of them, then the Kohathites would carry them, touching nothing more than the wrappings (vv. 15, 20).

2. The Gershonites (4:21-28). As in the case of the Kohathites above, this description centers on the duties of the Gershonites when the Tabernacle is to be moved. They are to carry the curtains of the Tabernacle and of the court around it.

3. The Merarites (4:29-33). This division is responsible for moving the structural framework of the Tabernacle. Since this was so heavy, wagons were assigned to the Merarites for their work (7:8).

4. Census of the Levites (4:34-49). In four short, repetitious paragraphs the result of the census of the working-age Levites is now given. Three paragraphs give the numbers of each of the three divisions, and the fourth gives the total. Verse 49 seems to mean that each man was appointed to a specific duty. So the work was well organized.

E. Miscellaneous Laws and Regulations (5:1–6:27)

One thing which can be noticed about the laws of this section is the way in which they fit the circumstances of a people in the wilderness, much of the time in temporary camping places. There is little or no obvious reason why these should be together.

1. Isolation of the Unclean (5:1-4). The purpose of this section is that the camp of the people of God must be kept hygienically and ceremonially clean. The Old Testament does not distinguish between the two kinds of cleanness. John Wesley is credited with saying that "cleanliness is next to godliness"; but the Pentateuch implies that "cleanliness is a part of godliness."

Three kinds of uncleanness were subject to isolation from the camp: lepers, persons with certain afflictions, and those who handled the dead. With our twentieth-century medical knowledge, we are able to distinguish better between those circumstances involving danger of contagion and those which do not. Such knowledge was not available in the time of Moses, so many forms of skin diseases were called leprosy, and all discharges were suspect, as was contact with any dead. In a group this size they could not take chances on spreading infection, and it was good sense to have rules such as these, even though the reason given is religious, and not expediency.

In the case of those who handled the dead, there were both religious and health reasons for the isolation. If the person had died with an infectious disease, there was danger of spreading it. This was the health reason. The religious reason was that the Israelites needed to break completely with pagan customs associated with death. For example, the Egyptians felt that the afterlife could not be happy unless the body was preserved from decay, so the body was very carefully preserved through a long process which involved much handling. It is almost as though God were telling the Israelites that they must consider the body as useless after death, and bury it as quickly as possible. Such passages as Leviticus 19:28 and Deuteronomy 14:1 also emphasize the break with pagan burial customs.

2. Restitution of Stolen Property (5:5-10). There is a law in Leviticus 6:1-7 which has to do with the restoration of stolen property. The present section is based on that law and expands it by giving a special application to a situation which could arise (v. 8). The former law made it clear that if anyone had stolen or defrauded, he must repay it, full value plus one-fifth, to the man from whom he had stolen. But the present passage tells what to do if the person who had been injured had died and there were no living relatives to receive payment in his place. In such a case, the thief could make his own heart right by paying the appropriate amount to the priest, as God's representative.

At first glance, this may seem to be simply a civil law, but there is a real spiritual truth here. It is assumed that any sin against man is also against God. This means that one must not only be right with his fellow man, but must make his peace with God also. So there is no such thing as sinning only against man. Every sin is a sin against God. This they learned early in their history as God's special people.

3. Ordeal of Jealousy (5:11-31). This is a strange and puzzling passage, and it is the only Biblical instance of trial by ordeal. The situation is that a woman is suspected of adultery, for which sin both the woman and the man involved are to be put to death (Lev. 20:10), but in this case there is no proof of the husband's suspicion and jealousy. So there is an unusually detailed description of the test which the woman is to undergo in order to decide her guilt or innocence. The whole thing seems very strange to us; it must have hinged on God's performing a miracle as proof of the truth. We have no record of its use.

This record does, however, emphasize both the need to keep the camp of the people of God clean from adultery, and the seriousness of jealousy.

4. Regulations for the Nazirites (6:1-21). The Hebrew word is *nazir*, which means "one who is separated, set apart." This differs strongly from the term Nazarene, which is applied to Jesus in Matthew 2:23. This chapter is the only full explanation of the Nazirites in the Old Testament. Samson is the only person who is called a Nazirite in the Old Testament (Judg. 13:5, 7, 13-14), though it is sure that Samuel was one (I Sam. 1:11), and such passages as Amos 2:11-12 shows that they were not uncommon in some periods.

One could be a Nazirite for a period of time or for life. He had three obligations: first, he must separate himself from the use of wine and strong drink, and from anything at all which derived from the grape vine; second, he must let his hair grow, thus making his difference apparent to all who see him; third, like the High Priest, he must not touch any dead body.

The usual practice was to make a vow to be a Nazirite for thirty days — according to rabbinic tradition. One might do this for a variety of reasons, such as thanksgiving, or as petition for something. Verses 13-21 describe the rites to be performed at the completion of the period of the vow.

5. The Priestly Blessing (6:22-27). These six verses deserve to be set apart in a chapter of their own, instead of being buried at

the end of a chapter of unrelated material. The blessing here given is one of the jewels of the Old Testament. Since this little, but beautiful blessing is to be pronounced by Aaron and his sons, it is called "The Priestly Blessing." The rabbis have protected this blessing by building around it a host of rules as to who could pronounce it, and how he must do so. One of the rules is that it must be done in the Hebrew language.

The blessing itself is found in the short verses 24, 25, and 26. In the Hebrew these consist of three, five, and seven words respectively. The rabbis feel that this is symbolic of the way in which the blessing progresses from petition for physical blessings to the highest blessing of all — peace. For they interpret verse 24 as meaning to bless with life, health, and prosperity, and to preserve from evil and temptation.

For God to *make His face to shine upon thee* (v. 25) means for Him to be friendly towards man, and also that He will provide salvation (cf. Ps. 80:19). For God to be *gracious* means both that He will show kindness and mercy, and that he will make one full of grace and lovable in the eyes of others. For God to *lift up His countenance upon thee* (v. 26) is for Him to turn His attention to you and to show you loving care.

Yet the climax of the whole blessing is in the petition that God may *give thee peace*. The Old Testament word *"peace"* (Heb. *shalom*) means far more than we often mean when we use it today. Even to list the meanings with which it is used in the Old Testament is instructive: The root meaning was "completeness, wholeness." But it was also used to mean: 2. Safety, security. 3. Welfare. 4. Health. 5. Prosperity, with needs filled. 6. Peace, quiet, tranquillity, contentment. 7. Peace from war. 8. Friendship, peace with others. 9. Peace with God. 10. Salvation.

Peace, then, is no mere negative freedom from war and strife. It is harmony with God and man. It is salvation from all that would hinder or harm. It is not mere peacefulness from outward trouble, but an inward state of the soul. No wonder that the ancient rabbis said that peace is one of the pillars of the world! It is easy, too, to see why *shalom* is still the universal greeting of the Jews, and is used both as "hello" and "goodbye."

F. The Princes' Offerings (7:1-88)

Chronologically, this chapter belongs after Leviticus 8, and before the Book of Numbers. But it is placed here because it included the bringing of supplies necessary for transporting the Tabernacle, which is one of the subjects under consideration in this first part of Numbers. The arrangement of much of Numbers is logical rather than chronological.

By *princes* is meant the heads of the tribes, as they are named in Numbers 1:5-15. Each of them presented the gift from his tribe, and the gifts were identical, to show that the tribes shared equally in responsibility. This is also stressed by means of the repetition of the same sentences in describing each of the gifts and its presentation.

First we are told that the twelve heads, or princes, of the tribes brought wagons and oxen to pull them, and gave them to the Levites. (vv. 1-9). These wagons and oxen were divided unevenly among the three divisions of Levites as the work of each division required. For example, since the Merarites had the heaviest materials to carry (Num. 4:31-32) they received four of the wagons. The Kohathites received none at all, since their job was to carry the vessels of the Tabernacle on their shoulders (4:1-15).

We are next told of the twelve gifts which were brought by the heads of the tribes for the dedication of the altar (vv. 10-83). These gifts are described in great detail, even though they were all exactly alike. They were brought and presented on successive days.

Verses 84-88 summarize the gifts and give the total of all that was brought on the twelve days, which was exactly twelve times what was brought by each. This fact stresses the importance of individual gifts, whether they are finer than others or not.

G. Miscellaneous Laws (7:89—10:10).

The verse which tells about God speaking to Moses (7:89) may have been originally connected with Chapter 7 or with Chapters 8 to 10. Or it may be displaced from its original connection, as some believe. But it is clearly not wrong to take it as introduction to what follows.

1. The Golden Lampstand (8:1-4). These verses are a footnote to Exodus 25, with the additional idea that the lamps must be so placed on the seven-branched lampstand that they throw the light forward (v. 3). This means that they would cast their light onto the north side of the Holy Place of the Tabernacle.

Not only is this a reminder that light is necessary. We are also reminded that the lamps had to be refilled every day and the wicks carefully trimmed. If we are to give light to the world (Matt. 5:14-16), we must keep ourselves in condition to give light all the time. This takes regular attention.

At this point it is not out of place to study the use Zechariah made of this symbolism (Zech. 4:1-14). He describes seeing in a vision such a lampstand, but with a difference. In his vision, there were two olive trees standing beside the lampstand; these were living sources of oil for burning, and were connected with pipes to the stand. In this way, the oil in the lamps was constantly renewed so that there was no danger of the lamps going out. Zechariah was told that this showed that the real source of light and power is in the Spirit of God. John, in turn, used the lampstand as a figure of the church (Rev. 1:20), which is supplied with the oil of the Spirit in an unending supply.

2. Purification and Presentation of the Levites (8:5-22). This passage is parallel to some extent to Leviticus 8 and Numbers 3:5-13. Yet this is not mere repetition; it is told here in such a way as to stress the difference between Levites and the common people of Israel. The section describes the way in which the Levites, in order to be ready to do their work in the Tabernacle, had to be cleansed physically and ceremonially. First there is the command that this be done (vv. 5-19) and then the account of the performance (vv. 20-22).

The command is given to separate the Levites from the children of Israel (vv. 6, 14) for their special work. This separation of the Levites for the work of the Tabernacle is presented as a great honor to them. They are separated *to the Lord* (v. 13) and they are to be His special possession (v. 14), in the place of the firstborn of all the tribes (v. 17; cf. 3:12-13). This is the first reason why they must be cleansed, since all that belongs to God must be clean, holy. The second reason is that it would be dangerous for them to go into the sanctuary without being cleansed (v. 19). The two reasons are closely related, since the sanctuary was sacred to God. It was not to be casually approached, nor must the furniture or vessels of the Tabernacle be casually handled or used. Only the Levites might handle these, and they must be specially sanctified for the purpose.

The preparation of the Levites for service included three elements: physical cleansing (v. 7), sin-offering (v. 8, 12), and commitment (vv. 9-10; 13). These three elements are in some form important in all Christian salvation.

The physical cleansing included shaving of all hair, washing the body, and washing the clothes. Only the "clean" thing or person was ready for the service of God, or fit to be dedicated to God. So before the Levites could be made holy (*qodesh* — "having a special relationship with God as a result of having been separated from common affairs and dedicated to Him"), they must first be cleansed (*tahor*) from all uncleanness (*tame'*) (see Appendix on "Holiness"). They had to be washed and shaved so as to remove any uncleanness, and their clothes were to be washed for the same reason. The uncleanness which is to be removed is that resulting from contact with anything unclean in any physical, ritual, or moral sense (see Appendix on "Holiness"). This concept of uncleanness is far different from that of our germ-conscious culture, but this should not disturb us too greatly. We must not seek to read our own concepts back into the Biblical record. We must rather seek to understand that the Hebrews, in the context of ancient Near Eastern culture, were seeking to relate themselves to a holy God, so as to respond effectively to His offer of a covenant relationship. They were to be His people, and He was to be their God. They were to do all in their power to be the kind of people He could accept. They knew that uncleanness was unacceptable to God. This would not be far from our saying that "cleanliness is next to godliness" except that they meant something far different by the word "unclean" than we mean. Their meaning was related to *mana* and *taboo* as ours is related to *sanitation* and *contagion*. Yet even as it would be wrong for us to minimize the cultural difference, so it would be wrong for us to fail to learn from the Hebrews because of that difference. We can learn that God demands purity. It is possible for us to have a higher concept and deeper knowledge of the meaning of the purity that God demands, but that fact does not negate the value of the earlier concept. The early Hebrews knew something of the requirements of God, and sought in their own way to meet them. If we know more about the requirements of God, then we must be all the more sure to live up to them.

Two offerings were made (v. 8): the first was a peace offering, or offering of praise to God (Lev. 3:1-5); and the second was the kind of sin offering which was prescribed for priests (Lev. 4:1-12). Only after these offerings could the Levites be fit for the service of the Tabernacle.

Then the Levites were to be dedicated to the service of the Lord (vv. 10-11). Verse 13, like 3:5-10, states that the Levites are to serve the priests, the sons of Aaron; but the emphasis here is on the fact that they are primarily serving the Lord. So they themselves are presented to the Lord as a wave offering (vv. 11, 13). The waving of an offering before the Lord was symbolic of its being given to Him (cf. Exod. 29:24-26; Lev. 7:30-34, etc.), but the waving of the Levites was probably symbolized either by them being led back and forth or by Aaron waving his hand before them. In any case, there is stress on the fact that they are being wholly given to the Lord (v. 14).

Verses 16-19 repeat the explanation of the Levites being taken by the Lord in the place of the firstborn of all Israel (3:11-13), and verses 20-22 state that the people did just as the Lord had commanded them.

3. Age Limits for Levites (8:23-26). It is stated here that the Levites are to serve in the Tabernacle from the ages of twenty-five to fifty. But in 4:3 it is stated they were not to begin service until thirty. Rabbinic tradition explains this by saying that they served a five-year apprenticeship before thirty. Later on the age was lowered to twenty (II Chron. 31:17; Ezra 3:8), probably because of different circumstances. Verse 25 describes retirement from the active work, but verse 26 shows that they were allowed to do limited tasks even after their compulsory retirement at fifty. The fact is that much of the work of the Levites, especially during a move, was heavy labor, and required both maturity and vigor. And even though some might be well able to serve past fifty, it was considered wise to have a rule which would be followed by all. Such is wisdom, and humanitarianism.

4. The Supplementary Passover (9:1-14). Note that this message from the Lord was given to Moses one month before the message recorded in the first chapter. Yet there is a special reason for the repetition of the instructions for the Passover given in Exodus 13. God has outlined the plans for travel and for the army. Now Moses must explain that everyone is to celebrate the Passover each year, even if other duties make it impossible for them to do so at the regular time. So the command to celebrate the Passover is given in verses 1-5, in order to make special provision for special cases.

In the repetition of the command to keep the Passover (vv. 1-5), there is emphasis on the care with which the ceremonies are to be observed (v. 3). The Passover celebrated their salvation from Egypt, which made it natural for John (19:36) to quote Numbers 9:12 and apply it to Christian salvation by showing that Jesus represents the true Lamb of the Passover. So it is well for us that the ceremonies were strictly kept. Much careful planning had to be done for so large a number to participate. Josephus says that not less than ten men joined together, with their families, and not more than twenty men. Each group would kill its lamb or two and carry out the rites and ceremonies.

Verses 6-8 present the special case of persons who were unclean because of their contact with a dead person whom they had buried, making it impossible for them to participate in the Passover in its regular annual celebration. This was an important problem, since every person who refused or neglected to participate was excommunicated (v. 13).

It was not a sin to touch a dead person, but it did render a person unfit for sacred ceremonies. This condition is described by the Hebrew word *tame'*, which is usually translated "unclean" in English. Uncleanness was not considered sinful, but was treated like sin, since it made a person unfit for service to God, at least temporarily (see Appendix on "Holiness").

When this problem was brought to Moses, he waited on God for the solution (v. 8). This solution called for another, supplementary Passover to be held one month later (v. 11) for those who could not participate in the first one. In this way, no one was omitted from this most important celebration. It is added (v. 10), that if any person missed the Passover because he was on a journey, he could also celebrate the second Passover. It is hard to see how there could be much, if any, need for this provision during the years they wandered in the wilderness, so this could be a later explanation.

Verse 13 does not clearly explain what the punishment for failing to keep the Passover was. It is not clear whether being *cut off from his people* (v. 13) means death or excommunication. In some cases excommunication would result in death. And in any case, it would mean being separated from the life of the whole people, and this, to the Hebrews, was as tragic as death.

Provision was always made for foreigners to be a part of the people of God (as in Exod. 12:45-49); now it is repeated that foreigners living among the people were to celebrate the Passover exactly like anyone else (v. 14). This is an example of the kind of Old Testament universalism of which most Christians seem unaware. The blessings of God have always been available for anyone who would meet the conditions and choose to accept them.

5. The Fiery Cloud (9:15-23). This section gives in more detail than does Exodus 40:34-38 the description of the cloud which covered the Tabernacle on the day of its dedication, and which led the people of God in all their wilderness wanderings. This record is presented as the firm assurance of Israel that in all of their wanderings, they were being daily led by God. Whatever scientific questions we may ask, we see this as one of the most important aspects of the whole history. As God leads us daily by the Holy Spirit, so He led Israel. Remove this guidance from the record, and there is no point to the story being told. It is not stated that they were guided *solely* by the cloud, but it is made abundantly clear that they were guided by God.

The cloud was dark in the day, and shone as fire in the night, in order to be visible both day and night. When it lifted up from the Tabernacle and moved forward, they followed after it. When it stopped, they made camp and waited for it to move again.

The account of the movements of the cloud strongly emphasizes the fact that God gave the orders and the people obeyed. No matter how long or short a time the cloud stood still, or how steadily it moved, they obeyed. They were to watch the cloud closely, and be ready at any time to follow the leading of God.

This illustrates for us the importance of following the leading of the Lord in all things. There is need for obedience. God knows far better than we do what is best for us and what is the wisest course for us to follow. Faith is also demanded. We must have faith that God not only can but will lead us through life, and that we are under His guidance and care.

The constant presence of the cloud by day and night was provided by God's infinite mercy. This new nation was in a strange land, in new circumstances, and without a long background of self-rule. They did not have a very good chance of setting up an independent government and proving themselves a free nation, humanly speaking. But the new nation was under the care and guidance of God. He gave them constant assurance of His watchful presence by means of the cloud. They could see it at any time and be assured that God was still with them. When they sinned, they may have wished for the time being that He would go away. But when they repented, they were happy that He was still with them.

Yet there is another side to the picture, and it would be wrong to neglect it. God has not made us automatons, and did not lead the people of Israel in a purely mechanical way. The constant reiteration of the words *at the commandment of the Lord* (vv. 18 twice, 20 twice, 23 three times) hints that something more was involved than the mere movement of the cloud. The last reference (v. 23) states that the commandment of the Lord was passed on to the people by means of Moses. And the very next section (10:1-10) describes a way which was used to pass on signals by which the people were to be guided. Chapter 11 tells of Moses asking Hobab, who knew the country through which they were to travel, to go with them and help them locate the best stopping-places. Chapter 13 tells of sending spies into Canaan to help them determine a course of action.

So the fact is that while God can and does lead us through the Holy Spirit, He does at the same time expect us to use the intelligence He gave us to evaluate various courses of action and choose what seems best. These facts are not contradictory; rather, they are two sides of one coin. It is neither God alone, nor man alone.

But God works with man, so long as man lets Him. Man must do the best he can with what wisdom he has, and trust God to work in and through his own wisdom and will to help him, ultimately, to do the will of God. Blessed is the man who eagerly seeks God's guidance as he seriously tries to reason out the best way to live.

6. The Silver Trumpets (10:1-10). Three kinds of trumpets are mentioned in the Old Testament, two of which were shaped like a ram's horn. But the kind described here is a tube about eighteen inches long, flared at one end. These were to be made of silver, each out of a single sheet. Two different pitches of trumpets were made, so that the people could tell whether one was being sounded, or two. Each could be sounded in more than one way, so that with two, a variety of calls was possible. Verse 2 gives two types of uses for the trumpets (calling assembly and summoning them to march), and verse 10 lists many others.

Four distinctly different signals are described in verses 3-7. Blowing both trumpets called the whole assembly together, meaning the representatives of all the families (v. 3). Blowing only one called together the heads of the tribes (v. 4). Blowing an alarm — a long blast of staccato notes — meant that the tribes camped on the east were to begin marching immediately (v. 5). A second alarm signaled the tribes on the south to begin marching. The Septuagint lists two more which are omitted here, and clearly states that a third and fourth alarm signalled for the tribes on the west and north to begin the journey.

Only the priests were to blow these trumpets (v. 8). The trumpets were to be used even after settling in Canaan (vv. 8-9). They were to be used on all special occasions (v. 10), in addition to the two special ways described previously. Verse 9 does not necessarily mean that the call of the trumpets would cause God to remember the people; rather, it would remind them that they were remembered of God.

II. SINAI TO PARAN (10:11—12:16)

This section describes the first of the three stages of travel from Sinai: Sinai to Paran, wilderness wanderings, Kadesh to Moab. The first section of the Book of Numbers can be viewed as appendices to the end of Exodus. Some of the events more briefly mentioned in Exodus are elaborated here. Some things in the first section had taken place prior to the dedication of the Tabernacle recorded in Exodus 40.

A comparison of Exodus 19:1 with Numbers 10:11 shows that the duration of the stay at Sinai was about eleven months. During that time they had received the Law twice, built and dedicated the Tabernacle, organized the camp, and celebrated the regular and special Passovers in memory of their deliverance from Egypt. Now they were ready to go on toward Canaan.

A. Departure from Sinai (10:11-36)

1. Time and Order of Departure (10:11-28). The whole trip is summarized briefly in verses 11-12, then the manner of departure is given in more detail in verses 13-28.

This journey was from Sinai to Paran. By this may be meant the large central wilderness of the Sinai Peninsula, though it is impossible to be accurate about the location of particular places in the wilderness. Tent dwellers do not leave the kinds of remains which would enable archeologists to identify places, and names change many times over the centuries. It is doubtful that we can even locate Sinai — scholars have suggested three widely separated mountains situated in the northern and southern parts of the Sinai Peninsula and east of the Gulf of Aqabah. The traditional site, Jebul Musa, in the southern tip of the Sinai Peninsula, has been so identified only since the fourth century A.D. Some have felt that it may have been near Kadesh-Barnea, in the northern part of the peninsula. Since it is impossible to be sure of this key location, it is hopeless to try to identify the less significant camping places.

Yet the Wilderness of Paran is considered to be a large area in the central and eastern peninsula. It may have included the Wilderness of Zin (not to be confused with the Wilderness of Sin — Exod. 16:1 — which was nearer Egypt). The chief camp in Paran was a place called Kadesh, or Kadesh-Barnea (cf. 13:26; 20:1). Modern travelers speak of this north-central area as the most fertile and best watered of the whole peninsula. It was here that the Israelites spent a generation before going on to Canaan (14:26-38).

It is interesting that when Moses retold this part of the story, he supplied a statement which is missing here: "You have remained long enough at this mountain; move on" (Deut. 1:6-7, An American Translation). So began their first journey after their stay at Sinai.

The manner of breaking camp and the order of marching follows almost exactly the details of Chapters 2 and 4. Once more the leaders of the various tribes are listed with the tribes. The Tabernacle was taken down and carried by the Levites on the wagons provided for this purpose (v. 17; cf. 7:5-9). Verse 17 regarding the position of the Levites seems to contradict 2:17. But verse 21 states that this was done so the heavier parts of the Tabernacle could be set up in the new camp before the Kohathites arrived with the furniture and vessels.

There were, no doubt, reasons for the particular order of march. But the important thing is that a system was followed and the work was not done haphazardly. Organization is more important than the form or manner of organization.

2. Moses' Father-in-law (10:29-32). A problem here is the identity of Hobab. He was either the father-in-law or brother-in-law of Moses. The evidence here and in Exodus 2 and 3 is so vague that either can be supported. To simplify the matter as much as possible, notice that three different names are ascribed to the *chothen* (father-in-law?) of Moses: Reuel or Raguel (Exod. 2:18), Jethro (Exod. 3:1), and possibly Hobab (Num. 10:29). Raguel and Reuel can very easily be two pronunciations of the same Hebrew name. It is possible that Jethro and Reuel are two names for the same man, the father-in-law of Moses, and that Hobab, the son, is Moses's brother-in-law. Or, Jethro and Hobab may be two names for the same man, and Reuel, the father of Jethro-Hobab, therefore the grandfather-in-law of Moses, in which case, either of them might be called *chothen* in Hebrew. The fact that Exodus 18:27 tells of Jethro leaving the Israelites leads some to feel that Hobab was his son and that he remained with them. Rabbinic tradition considers Hobab and Jethro the same man, Moses' father-in-law, and Reuel the father of Jethro-Hobab, Moses' grandfather-in-law.

Moses asked Hobab, who was acquainted with all the country, to go with the Israelites and help them find the best camping-places (v. 31). The story is incomplete, as the answer of Hobab is not given; but if he had not gone on with them, there would have been no reason to include the story. The conclusion that

Hobab did go with them is supported by Judges 1:16; 4:11.

This is an interesting conversation, in which Moses is asking for human guidance. We had previously been told about the guidance of the fiery cloud (9:15-23), and are reminded of this later in verse 34. Verse 33 is obscure, but seems to describe divine guidance. Why would Moses ask for Hobab to serve as guide? It has been suggested above (on 9:15-23) that we have here a balance suggested between the two extremes of depending on God without trying to use human wisdom, and depending on human wisdom alone. One is almost as foolish as the other. God intended for man to use all of his God-given powers of wisdom, foresight, and experimentation to seek out the best ways of life. But God never intended for man to depend only on his own powers. God provides guidance which goes beyond man's ability, and the wise man will eagerly seek to understand such guidance.

This reminds us that the guidance of the Lord has never at any time in history been as simple to follow as we wish it were. We tend to feel that in "Bible times" God made His will so clear by means of audible voices, dreams, visions, etc., that there was never any doubt at all about what God wanted. It is not that simple for us. And it was not that simple for such men as Moses. We are told more than eighty times in the Book of Numbers alone, that God spoke to Moses, yet it is never as clear as we would like just *how* He spoke. (See 12:4-10 for a discussion of this point.)

When Moses said *we will do thee good,* he must have been promising Hobab a portion of land in the land of Canaan to which they were going.

3. Movements of the Ark (10:33-36). Some translations seem to imply that the Ark moved of its own accord, so this is pointed to as an example of ancient folklore of little or no historical value. This literalness seems excessive and unnecessary. The Ark was carried about by the Levites, usually in the midst of the people. Rabbi Ibn Ezra says that this one time (v. 33) the Ark was carried in front of the procession, in order to inspire the people with confidence and courage.

There is also no reason to take the phrase *three days journey* as meaning that the Ark went that far ahead of the people. At this point King James Version makes clear the idea that in the three days journey, the Ark went ahead of them as they sought for a place to camp.

Verses 35-36 have a special significance to the Jews, and they are still quoted at a certain point in each synagog service. Some of the rabbis, in fact, thought of this tiny section as a separate Book of the Torah. These two verses, sometimes called the "Song of the

Ark," are the invocation prayers which Moses prayed at the beginning and end of a journey, as the Ark was picked up and set down. The Ark was a sign of the guarding presence of the Lord going with His people to guide and protect them.[1] These prayers of invocation were said each time the Ark was taken up and set down. In modern synagogs they are said each time the Torah is taken out of the "ark" or replaced there. The first is a prayer for victory over enemies, and the second is a prayer for the blessing of the Lord on His own people.

B. Various Incidents (11:1-35)

1. Complaints at Taberah (11:1-3). Here we turn to one of the recurring themes of the story of the wilderness wanderings — the murmuring of the people against Moses and against God. It is a shock to read first of the guidance of God in the end of the tenth chapter and straight into the eleventh chapter and this story of complaining. But that is the way people are. The same people can be full of joy and faith, and then so quickly turn against their leaders and against God, becoming doubtful and suspicious. Every pastor and teacher needs to know that, and guard against depending too much on the support of those with whom he is working.

It is true that the people had been wonderfully delivered from Egypt, and had been greatly blessed with God's leadership. But they were human, and the day-to-day business of living caused some of them to murmur against Moses and against God. The *fire of the Lord* which began suddenly in tents at the edge of the camp may have been caused by lightning or some other unexplained cause. It soon caused the people who had complained to call for Moses to pray for them. So they remembered this place by the Hebrew word for "burning."

2. Complaints about Manna (11:4-10.) This story moves forward on two levels simultaneously: The complaining of the people followed by God's answer and their punishment, and the lament of Moses and God's plan for assistance. It begins in this section with the complaint of the people.

[1] The Ark was very closely associated with the presence of God. There are scholars who believe that it was originally worshiped as God, or as the actual dwelling place of God, and use such passages as this as evidence, saying that it comes close to equating God and the Ark. The use of the Ark in battle (I Sam. 4:3-22) is also pointed out as supporting this interpretation. Yet the whole tenor of the Old Testament teaching about the nature of God is so opposed to this that we must reject that conclusion. If the Israelites ever thought of the Ark as more than a symbol of God's presence, that concept has been obliterated from the Old Testament.

The mixed multitude (v. 4) is that group of aliens who left Egypt with the Israelites (Exod. 12:38). They were given this rather contemptuous designation because they were composed of unrelated families of uncertain ancestry. The rebellion started with these people, but quickly spread throughout the camp. The people had a strong craving for meat, such as they had had in Egypt. They were tired of the monotony of manna and were eager for a change of diet. Instead of being grateful for the miraculously provided food, they began to complain and to murmur. Like children, they were soon weeping for what they could not have.

Fish were said to be cheap in Egypt, easily available as it was from both the Mediterranean Sea and the Nile. Even the poorest of the people could have fish in Egypt. In fact, all of the foods they mention in this verse are those which, because of their abundance, were inexpensive. But they are also the strong-flavored foods and spices which were quite different from the blandness of the daily manna. It was not merely that the people longed for meat; they wanted the *leeks, and the onions, and the garlic,* which had so strongly flavored all their food in Egypt.

Concentration on the cravings they could not satisfy led to the wild exaggeration of verse 6. The people were not starving to death, as they pretended, for God was supplying their daily needs. But when once started, the complaining grew so that soon they could see nothing but the troubles of that day. They could not remember the blessings they had been enjoying for so long. The cheap onions and garlic and fish of which they had had such meager portions in Egyptian slavery were magnified by their imagination into royal banquets. By the same token, the sameness of their daily manna, provided by God's mercy, faded into nothing. They could not enjoy the present for thinking of the past. No wonder this childish attitude displeased God so greatly.

Verses 7-9 are a parenthetical explanation about manna, which is here mentioned for the first time in the Book of Numbers (cf. Exod. 16:5-35). We know nothing about manna except what is told us here and in Exodus. The speculation that the word refers to the sugary Tamarisk sap, assumes that the Biblical description is unhistorical and romanticized.

Verse 10 returns to the weeping of the people, which was general and unconcealed — *every man in the door of his tent!* Both Moses and God were angry at this display. The Bible does not hesitate to ascribe wrath to God, but by this it never means blind human passion. Wrath is rather the settled attitude of God toward sin, which cuts man off from His love and mercy. God's love demands that He seek by every means to turn man from his rebellion so that man might live. So God's love may at times look so much like wrath that no other word will describe it; yet it is still everlasting love — even if man rebels to the end and forever cuts himself off from God's love.

3. Moses' Expostulation with Yahweh (11:11-15). It is not surprising that Moses was disturbed at the weeping and complaining throughout the camp. Who would not be? Worn down by the cares of leading such a crowd, and by their murmuring attitude, he felt for the moment that it was too much for him. If this was what leadership was like, he would be happy to die right then! Besides that, he knew there was no way to answer the demand of the people for meat.

4. Yahweh's Reply to Moses (11:16-24a). Before dealing with the demand for meat, God told Moses what to do about his own personal problem. For a large part of Moses' difficulty was that, like most leaders, he was trying to carry too much of the load himself. As a consequence he was worn down physically and emotionally, which in turn impaired his leadership abilities.

God told Moses to choose seventy elders of the people who were known by him to be leaders, and respected by the people. God would give them each a share of the Holy Spirit, so that they could share in the responsibility of leadership. Something like this had been done at the urging of Jethro (Exod. 18:13-25), but this group had a more spiritual purpose. The first group were administrators with delegated authority. These men were to share with Moses the burden of the spiritual leadership of the people. This would alleviate the emotional strain on Moses. (What a blessing this would be for a pastor!) By saying that God would *"take of the Spirit which is upon thee, and will put it upon them"* (v. 17), God was not saying that Moses would have any less of the Spirit, but that the Spirit of God that would rest on the seventy would be exactly like the blessing of Moses. There is no historical connection between this group and the Sanhedrin, which dates from the second or third century before Christ.

God now turns to the problem of the meat, and tells Moses to call upon the people to *sanctify* themselves — fit themselves for the blessing of God. They were near the point of rebellion and needed to make themselves spiritually, emotionally, and physically fit to receive God's blessing. God promised not merely to give them meat, but to give them so much that they would eat it for a month and come to loathe it! The tone of God's promise signifies that God was giving them what they wanted, but not what they needed. What they wanted was not good for them, and though they thought of it as a blessing to be longed for, it was really a plague (Ps. 106:15). Moses was astonished at such an answer; he could not conceive how so much meat could be supplied.

5. Eldership and Prophecy (11:24b-30). God put His Spirit upon the seventy, and *they prophesied*. This probably does not mean that they predicted anything, though that *could* be a part of prophesying. More probably they taught, preached, and exhorted the people with divine authority. The final phrase of verse 25 is most correctly translated, "and no more." It could not mean what the King James Version says ("and did not cease"). The implication seems to be that this was a special occasion, and that God took care of the emergency by enabling these men to prophesy temporarily, so as to bring the people to some point of obedience.

Verse 26 states that two of the seventy had declined to come to the Tabernacle with the others, and had remained in the camp. Nevertheless they too began prophesying under the inspiration of the Spirit. When word of this was brought to Joshua, he was deeply disturbed, and called on Moses to stop them, possibly fearing that this would detract from the authority of Moses. Now, Moses had just displayed his human weakness by becoming so discouraged, but in his answer to Joshua he rose to one of the highest peaks of his life. He declared his desire that *all* of the people might be filled with the Spirit and prophesy! He refused to be jealous.

6. The Supply of Meat (11:31-35). The people had demanded meat; now God supplied an abundance of it. Quails migrate between Africa and Syria twice a year; travelers still tell of their being caught in great abundance at certain times and places. We are told here of a strong wind which caused the tired birds to fly into the camp at a height of about three feet above the ground, so that the people could rather easily knock the birds down. They killed them and spread the meat in the sun to cure. But some of them gorged themselves on the raw meat. It may be that this was the cause of the plague, or it may be some other cause. At any rate, large numbers died and were buried there. Hence the name, *Graves-of-craving*.

C. Miriam, Aaron, and Moses (12:1-16)

After the rebellion of the whole people, Moses now had to deal with the more serious rebellion of his only sister and his only brother against his leadership. They had been jealous before, but became even more so after the special honor God had shown

Moses just before this (11:16-17). This event is the occasion of very important statements about divine revelation which we must seek to understand.

1. Complaint against Moses (12:1-2). One's leadership is never tested more severely than when rebellion comes from the relatives and closest associates of the leader. Miriam and Aaron brought two accusations against Moses: That he had married *a Cushite woman*, and that he had assumed an unwarranted monopoly over divine communications. The first accusation is puzzling for several reasons. We do not know of any recent marriage of Moses. We cannot certainly identify the meaning of *Cushite*. If this was Zipporah, why did they wait until this time to complain? In any case, this accusation was not mentioned again, and all that follows concentrates on the second accusation. This first accusation may have been only an excuse, and a poor one, for attacking Moses.

The real accusation against Moses was that he assumed he was primarily the one through whom the word of God was given to the people. This was no real cause for complaint, since both Miriam and Aaron also had places of highest honor among the people. Miriam had been called a "prophetess" (Exod. 15:20), and Aaron was Moses' spokesman. Yet it was clear that Moses was first in leadership, and his older brother and sister grew discontented with second place. They began to covet this position of leadership, and started a campaign to get it by force.

2. The Meekness of Moses (12:3). Those who support the direct Mosaic authorship of the whole Book of Numbers find this to be a major difficulty, though not an insoluble one. There is no problem if we assume that, though the basic material is from the time of Moses, the Book did not assume its final form until much later.

The idea expressed here is that Moses was not grasping for power, so he took no steps to defend himself. He did not answer the charge, but swallowed his hurt and took the matter to the Lord. In this, he showed his greatness, and his qualification for his place of leadership. No spiritual leader should fight for a position, or fight to hold his position.

3. Moses' Vindication (12:4-10). This rebellion on the part of two leaders of the people was of such serious consequence that God found it necessary to use unusual means to quell it. Appearing to Moses alone would reassure him, but would do nothing to change the attitude of Miriam and Aaron. God therefore chose

to appear visibly and unexpectedly to all three of them at the same time. He did so in the forecourt of the Tabernacle. The meaning of verse 5 seems to be that the cloud separated Miriam and Aaron from Moses so as to set him apart from them. God then spoke to the three of them in no uncertain terms. Such drastic action was necessary at this time, since the action of Miriam and Aaron came immediately after a serious rebellion on the part of the people. This was a crisis of Moses' leadership.

God did not say whether Miriam and Aaron ever received messages from Him or not. He simply pointed out that Moses was in a superior position over all other prophets. God might speak to other prophets by means of a vision or a dream, but with Moses He speaks *face to face*, literally, *mouth to mouth*. That is, God spoke with Moses in a way which was more personal, direct, and unmistakable (cf. 7:89).

God actually is saying (v. 7) that Moses is high above all other prophets. He thus places Moses and his revelations above all others, before Christ. In a very real sense, then, the Mosaic Law is the foundation of the whole Old Testament, and the Jews were right to always honor it above all the rest. It is because of this statement that Hebrews 3:1-6 speaks so highly of Moses. But notice that the passage in Hebrews draws a contrast between Moses as a *servant* of God, and Jesus as His *Son*.

Consider now the ways in which God revealed His will to man in the Old Testament. If we exclude the world of nature, which tells about God, but not about His will, we have five ways: Personal appearance, angel (Christ?), dream, vision, and word. Of these, the last is most common. But this does not necessarily mean an audible word. The Hebrew *davar* means not only a verbal message, but also a thing, event, or act. The Old Testament speaks more than 4000 times of the "word of the Lord" coming to man (138 times in Numbers!), but seldom speaks of the *way* in which the word was communicated. Further consideration must be given to the place of the Holy Spirit in revelation (11:25-29). Moses received the word of God because the Holy Spirit rested upon him, and the same is true of all others in the Old Testament.

The fact is that though we tend to glamorize the ancient past, and wish that God would work with us as He did with the ancients, God has used much the same methods in all ages. The same Holy Spirit who talked with Moses and the prophets can speak daily to us. One difference is that in the Old Testament the Spirit usually came only to special persons or in special times, but He now comes upon all Christians in a continuous abiding presence. We do not appreciate and utilize to the fullest the blessings God makes available to us.

Verse 9 means that God made clear His anger, and then closed the interview. It appears that Miriam especially was singled out for punishment, possibly indicating that she was the instigator of the trouble, for when the cloud lifted, she was seen to be a leper. This required her banishment from the camp.

4. Moses' Intercession for Miriam (12:11-16). Aaron, having been strongly rebuked by the word of God, addressed Moses as his superior and pleaded for Moses to intercede for their sister. He admitted that both of them had sinned. Too bad he had not been strong enough to resist Miriam in the first place! Aaron here shows the weakness of character which prevented him from being the kind of leader he coveted being. He was fluent in speech, but this was not enough.

Once more Moses showed his greatness of character and his meekness. He had nothing against those who had sought to usurp his position, and he refused to hold a grudge. He immediately responded to the plea of Aaron by praying earnestly for Miriam. The prayer is eloquent in its brevity.

Apparently God answered Moses' prayer and healed Miriam at once, though the text does not say so. God said that she would have to be put out of the camp for seven days, which was the period of isolation prescribed of one who had been cleansed (cf. Lev. 14:8). So the people waited at Hazeroth for the seven days, and while Miriam went through the ceremonies of purification described in Leviticus 14. These rites are not mentioned here as they were well known. They went then to Kadesh, in the wilderness of Paran.

III. IN PARAN (13:1–19:22)

A. The Spies (13:1–14:45)

This section marks a turning point in the travels of the Israelites. They had now arrived at the southern boundary of the promised land of Canaan. If all had gone well, they would have been at the end of their journey. But instead, they were timid enough to send spies into the land to look it over, then accepted the majority report of the spies and decided tearfully that they were not able to enter the land and settle there. God then condemned them to wandering nearly thirty-eight years in the wilderness. Only those who were then children and who did not participate in the decision refusing to enter into the land, only these were to be allowed to see the promised land. The others were to die in the wilderness.

One wonders what would have happened if the people had been willing to believe the report of Caleb and Joshua. The whole history of Israel would have been different. But when the people rejected the best plan God could make for them, they had to take God's second-best. In the same way, if we reject God's best, we get God's second-best.

1. Appointment of Twelve Spies (13:1-17a). The record here simply states that God ordered the sending of the spies, but Deuteronomy 1:19-24 says that the people asked to be allowed to send them, and that Moses approved the plan. Actually, the plan to send out spies showed commendable forethought; the trouble came after the return.

Note that each tribe was to be represented by a leader going to see the land. This is one of the many examples of the systematic way God was teaching the people to operate their affairs. Probably these men should be called "scouts," as *spies* has connotations in our age which should not be applied to those men.

The names of the men are given. These names, which give every sign of being from the period of Moses, indicate their authenticity. Note that Joshua is first called Hoshea (v. 8), and then it is explained in verse 16 that that had been his name originally, but that Moses had changed it to *Yehoshua*, which is now usually spelled *Joshua* in English, and *Jesous* in Greek (cf. Acts 7:45; Heb. 4:8). The first name means "He has helped," or "saved." The name Moses gave to him means "The Lord has saved."

2. Briefing of the Spies (13:17b-20). Moses told them to go up into the land and learn some specific things about it. They were to see what kind of land it was, and what kind of people lived there. Were they nomads, living in tents? Or were they settled in strong cities which protected them? What kind of food grew in the land? Was there plenty of wood available for fuel? And they were to bring back a sample of whatever fruit of the land might be in season. (Judging from the end of v. 20, it was about the last of July or the first of August.)

3. The Territory Surveyed (13:21-24). The spies, or scouts, traversed the whole length of the land, from the southern border to the foot of Mount Hermon, near the sources of the Jordan River.[2] Rehob was the farthest north. *Sons of Anak* is equivalent to *Anakim*, and apparently means unusually tall men. They are mentioned several times in Deuteronomy and Joshua, and once in Judges. Hebron, south of Jerusalem, later became the first capital city of David.

To cover so much territory in forty days was not easy. They may have split into groups so as to cover the territory faster.

4. The Spies' Return to Paran (13:25-26a). The term "forty days" which occurs so often in Scripture may not necessarily mean a certain number of days. (*Forty days* is found fourteen times in the Old Testament, and *forty years,* thirty-one times.)

5. The Spies Report (13:26b-33). In verses 27-29, the ten give their majority report. "*It floweth with milk and honey,*" they said, using an old expression for a fertile land (cf. Exod. 3:8). After more than a year in the wildernesses of the Sinai Peninsula, Canaan looked good to them! Some think this indicates that the land was more fertile at that time than it is now. But the ten spies probably exaggerated the fertility of the land just as they exaggerated the size of the inhabitants and the dangers which were in the land.

To the Israelites, who were shepherds and who lived in tents, the settled cities with walls around them must have seemed absolutely impregnable. They had helped to build heavy-walled fortresses in Egypt, and knew how safe they made the inhabitants.

The country was at this time inhabited by a variety of peoples,

[2]Since their instructions said nothing about going so far, many scholars assume that two divergent stories have been woven together, one from J and one from P, and that the combination has been expanded. That such a complex history of the text is unnecessary is clearly shown by the thorough discussion of the problems involved by A. A. MacRae, "Numbers," *New Bible Commentary.*

of which the Hittites and Amorites had been sole rulers at different times. The Canaanites were now the chief people in the land, and gave their name to it. The Philistines had come by ship and settled along the southern seacoast on the plains. (Much later the whole land was called *Palestine,* which means "the land of the Philistines." *Palestine* is used several times in the King James Version, but should not be interpreted in the modern sense.) The Amorites lived along the Jordan, and the Hivites and the Perizzites were located in the mountains of both the north and the south.

In their report the scouts enumerated the various races of people in order to make it sound as bad as possible, for they had already decided they should not try to take the land. Since their mind was made up, they tried to present a persuasive report — one-sided.

Caleb interrupted the report at this point and urged an immediate push forward into this land, insisting that they were more than ready for the conquest. Such courage was needed, but he was not able to overcome the discouraging report of the other spies.

Notice that no real facts or figures are presented by either side. Caleb expresses his faith, and the other men express their doubt, and that is all there is to it. But it takes a lot of faith to overcome such doubt as these men expressed, especially when the people had already shown themselves to be easily discouraged. In spite of the miracles God had performed for them, they were constantly on the point of giving up and going back to Egypt.

Verse 33 is interesting and instructive. When one thinks he looks small or insignificant in the eyes of others, he looks small to himself.

6. Israel's Complaints (14:1-2). Imagine the pitiful sight of the whole congregation spending the night in wakeful weeping because of the discouraging report which they had accepted! There was no excuse for this disgraceful behavior, for God had promised to lead them into the land successfully, just as He had led them this far. After all that God had done for them in the last year or more, how could they possibly doubt His power now? But they did. They were childish.

All of this demonstrates that each new struggle requires new faith, new courage, and new grace that only God can supply.

The lament in verse 2 shows the forgetfulness of depression. The people were so discouraged about the future that they looked back to their days of slavery with longing! They even thought it would be better to die in the wilderness than to be killed in Canaan!

7. Design for Retreat (14:3-4). It is not sinful to ask why God permits certain troubles or problems, providing one is asking in the right spirit. The Israelites, however, were asking in disbelief and strong doubt. In spite of the fact that God had told them all along of His purpose for them, and had assured them that He would do for them all that needed to be done, the people would not believe when anything at all threatened them.

One is tempted to say that there was no excuse at all for their attitude and fear. It is true that they were a newly freed nation, and that they had not yet had a long history of working together, and had never before tried to take over a hostile land. It is also true that all of these people had grown up in a heathen land, among idol worshipers. But they themselves had been taught all their lives to worship God and trust Him. And they had been taught all their lives that God was going to deliver them from their bondage and take them back to the land which had been promised to the descendants of Abraham.

So it is astonishing that they would want to go back to Egypt. All of their lives they, and their parents, and their grandparents had wanted to leave Egypt and go to the land of promise. They had longed with all their hearts to get away from the hard slavery and terrible treatment of the Egyptians. They had prayed every day for God to deliver them from that.

And now they were asking to go back to Egypt — to the old slavery. All the blessings of the past two years, and all the opportunity which lay ahead of them, all this was forgotten in their discouragement and unbelief. Rather than try something new, they wanted to return to the worst they had ever known. The trouble of the present made the past troubles fade from their minds, so that they could remember only the few good things they had enjoyed in Egypt. And they wanted to go back.

8. Report of Caleb and Joshua (14:5-9). Overwhelmed by sorrow and shame, Moses and Aaron fell on their faces before the people and before God. Joshua and Caleb tore their cloaks in the age-old sign of bereavement. It was an expression of the proper attitude in the face of the discouragement and doubt of the people. Then they made their appeal to the people to reconsider. First, they reminded the people that the land was a good land (v. 7), and second, that the Lord was well able to deliver the land to them if they would only trust Him and obey. (The second part

of v. 9 is puzzling, but certainly means that taking the land will be easy, with God's help.)

9. Tragedy Averted (14:10). Now the discouragement of the people turned to open rebellion, and they prepared to stone their leaders. It was neither the first nor the last time that leaders appointed by God were so turned against. This shows the depth of the apostasy of the people.

It was at this point that God appeared to them in the cloud, and put a stop to the demonstration. The crisis called for stringent measures.

10. God's Threat and Moses' Intercession (14:11-25). God says that He will cause all these rebellious people to die, and then will build a new nation out of Moses. God had said this once before, when the people had sinned so greatly at Sinai (Exod. 32:10). In a sense, this is just what happened, for all the rebellious people died, and another generation entered the land of promise.

Now Moses rises from his despondency to intercede for the people (vv. 13-19). He raises two objections to the plan of God: first, he declares that if the people fail to go on into Canaan, Egypt and other nations will hear about it and conclude that Yahweh is a feeble god among their own gods. Second, he asks God to demonstrate His eternal nature of mercy by forgiving the sin of the people. He quotes God's own words about Himself (v. 18; cf. Exod. 34:6-7).

God answers that He has already forgiven the people. Moses did not have to tell God to be like Himself. He had already answered the prayer; yet it was good for Moses to pray as he did. How many of our prayers have already been answered before we voice them?

Yet God insists that His forgiving the people does not change their fate. The glory of God must be vindicated, and will be, by the demonstration of His power in leading a people into the land of promise (cf. Ezek. 36:16-23). But it will not be all of these people, for the adults who disobeyed must die in the wilderness, then their children will enter into the land by the power of God.

There is no escaping the fact that sin has consequences. And even the forgiveness of God does not always allow one to avoid these consequences.

11. Yahweh's Punishment Pronounced (14:26-38). God here spells out the doom of the people who have rebelled so grievously and irrevocably. He tells them that He will not help them go on, but will let them die in the wilderness. This is partly punishment

administered by God, and partly the inevitable consequence of their lack of courage. So it is often in life, both with individuals and with groups. Many a pastor rejects the challenge of his congregation and moves on to another, never knowing what might have been if he had had faith and courage to persist. Then, another does what he could have done.

12. Attempted Invasion Defeated (14:39-45). The shock of their doom stirred the people to a most tragic attempt to reverse it. They suddenly and defiantly decided that they would enter the land anyway. Not only did they refuse to ask God to go with them, neither would they listen to Moses who tried to show them how foolishly they were acting. This abortive and ill-advised battle was doomed before it began. They suffered a crushing defeat. Nothing now was left for them but to do what God had told them would be their punishment — wander in the wilderness for the rest of their lives.

B. Miscellaneous Laws (15:1-41)

Chapters 15 through 19 tell all we know about the events of the thirty-eight years of "wandering," and that is next to nothing. It is as though these years of disgrace and lack of progress were better forgotten. The only major event described is the sedition of Korah (chap. 16). Various laws are described, which are to be kept after the people enter the land of Canaan, so it appears that to some extent the minds of the people were directed to the future. We are left with a host of questions about the events of these years, which are nowhere answered.

1. Flour, Oil, and Wine for Sacrifice (15:1-16). This is so much like the instructions of Leviticus 1–7 that there seems little need for the repetition. It may be that it was a means of directing the minds of the people toward the time when God would fulfill His promise and take them into the land where they were to keep these laws.

Leviticus 2:1-11 had already described the way in which "meat" (food) should be offered with every burnt offering. This section specifies the amounts of food which shall be offered with each kind of sacrifice, and also stresses the idea that this is to be *a pleasing odor to the Lord* (vv. 3, 7, 10, 13, 14, R.S.V.). Note how the same phrase is applied to the self-sacrifice of Jesus (Eph. 5:2), and to the good works of Christians (Phil. 4:18).

One further point can be noticed about the food offering. It was of grain, which requires more human labor for production and preparation than does an animal. Even after the grain is grown, it must be threshed, ground and prepared, so it represents the labor of the person, as the animal of sacrifice represents the person himself. God demands that we give Him ourselves, and the fruits of our labor.

The section concludes by stressing once more that the same rule applies to all, whether native Israelite or converted foreigner (vv. 15-16).

2. Offerings of Coarse Meal (15:17-21). The point of this obscure passage seems to be that the housewife must give to God the first of every batch of bread she bakes. This is in addition to the giving of the first of the grain as it is threshed, and teaches the stewardship of all things. *Heave offering* (*terumah*) means "*gift.*"

3. Offerings for Unknown Sins (15:22-29). Leviticus 4 also describes sacrifices for sins done in ignorance. This section distinguishes between sins of the congregation and sins of an individual. It is instructive for us to note that sin must be atoned for, even if one does not learn until later that he has done wrong. The Bible never takes sin lightly, but does say it can be forgiven.

4. Punishment of Defiant Sinners (15:30, 31). Verses 30-31 describe the other extreme — the sin which a person commits in open defiance — *with a high hand.* Such a sin made the person unfit to be a part of the covenant people of God, so he had to be put to death.

5. A Sabbath Breaker's Fate (15:32-36). This is an example of the kind of defiant sin which has just been mentioned (vv. 30-31). The punishment prescribed (Exod. 31:14-15) is death, but the manner of execution had not been mentioned. The decision that he is to be stoned is then carried out. This seems drastic to us, but we can at least note that the death was not revenge of a person, but justice carried out by the whole people, in a solemnly prescribed ceremony. In this it does not differ from modern executions, except that we delegate certain persons to do the act. But there must be a way, with our knowledge of the grace and mercy of Jesus Christ, and the work of the Holy Spirit, for us to learn to be more redemptive in our treatment of criminals!

6. Wearing Tassels (15:37-41). As the Christians use the symbols of the cross, the fish, or the yoke, so the Hebrews were given the tassel on their clothing, to remind them of their heritage, and of the commandments of God. Orthodox Jews today still wear the tallith at certain times, though they discontinued wearing

fringed garments all the time by the thirteenth century A.D.

C. Rebellion of Korah, Dathan, and Abiram (16:1–17:13)

There is no indication of the time of these events, except that they happened sometime during the thirty-eight years between the sending of the scouts and the move into Canaan. Probably it was neither near the beginning nor the end of that period.

The chapter is complex, difficult to outline, and leaves unanswered questions in our minds. This is because the events themselves were exceedingly complex. It was not a simple uprising on the part of a well-defined group. It was open rebellion on the part of two groups, for different reasons; and both groups had many supporters among the people in general. It is a miracle that Moses did not lose control completely. God intervened in a way which left an indelible impression on all.

1. The Rebels (16:1-2). There were two groups of rebels: Korah and his group rebelled against the exclusive priesthood of Aaron and his sons. Dathan and Abiram rebelled against the leadership of Moses. So we have both religious rebellion and political rebellion at the same time. This accounts in part for the complexity of the chapter.

Dathan and Abiram were from the tribe of Reuben, descendants of the eldest son of Jacob. They felt that for this reason they should be the leaders. They had a large number of leading and respected men on their side. This was mutiny.

2. Korah's Rebellion (16:2-11). Korah, knowing well how to win support for his cause, posed as the champion of the people against the establishment. He declared that Moses was taking upon himself too much authority, since all the people were holy and had God with them. He took this half-truth and used it to stir up rebellion. Such has always been the way of those who would be leaders at any cost.

Korah's claim is that since he and others are of the tribe of Levi, they ought to be priests as well as the sons of Aaron. Moses, deeply disturbed at this charge (v. 4), tells Korah and the others to let God decide for all of them who had the right to be priests. Moses does not so much make a bold challenge, as suggest to Korah and his followers that they test their acceptability before God to be priests by attempting one of the minor tasks of priests (vv. 5-7).

Moses then reminds the Levites who are rebelling that God has already given them much honor in setting them apart to do the service of the Tabernacle for the priests (vv. 8-11). He reminds them that it is the Lord Himself who has chosen the priests, not Aaron or Moses, so that it is the Lord they are really opposing (v. 11). In this way, Moses put the discussion on the proper level.

3. Revolt of Dathan and Abiram (16:12-15). When Moses sends for these two rebels against his political leadership, they refused to come (v. 12). Notice how they refer to Egypt as though it were the wonderful place where they all ought to be (v. 13). They also accuse Moses of setting himself up as an absolute monarch (*altogether a prince*). The third accusation is ridiculous — that he has not provided rich *fields and vineyards* here in the wilderness! The fourth charge is that Moses wants to blind the people to the true facts by his smooth words.

Moses' answer to the charges is to pray that God will not accept the offering they will make on the next day. He further states that he has not acted like the despot they accuse him of being, for he has neither taken anything from them nor hurt them.

4. Ordeal of Korah (16:16-24). Moses here warns Korah and his followers that they must not fail to come the next day to put to the test their serious charges. And so they did. They prepared to carry in their censers holy fire from the Tabernacle, which none but the priests were to handle.

A divine manifestation met them and God warned the innocent to separate themselves from the rebels for their own protection. The rebellion of the people had gone so far that drastic action was necessary if the people of God were to be saved. God prepared to take that action.

5. Ordeal of Dathan and Abiram (16:25-34). Verse 27 states that after all the people separated themselves from them, Korah and his companions, Dathan and Abiram came and stood defiantly in their tent doors. This shows the depth of their degradation and the strength of their stubborn rebellion. Such could not go unpunished — considering the temper of the rest of the people. Too many were sympathetic.

Moses, led by the Spirit of God, made a bold declaration that these wicked men would not die a natural death, and that their dramatic death would vindicate his leadership. This would show that Moses had not made himself leader, but that he had been made so by God. Moses even said that God would create a *new thing* (v. 30), which is a strong Hebrew expression for what we would call a *miracle*. This is exactly what happened when the earth opened up in a miraculous earthquake, and closed over the rebels after they had fallen in (vv. 32-33).

6. Further Punishment (16:35-50). Those who were seeking to be priests were unlawfully carrying holy fire, and the fire of God consumed them. In order not to cause any more trouble, Moses had the sacred fire emptied from the censers, and warned that the censers were now dedicated to God by having carried the fire (v. 37). They could no longer be used for secular purposes, so they were beaten into sheets for a covering for the Altar (v. 38). All who saw them afterwards would remember the story and be warned that no stranger to the priesthood should ever try to do the work of a priest (v. 40).

The extent of the rebellion is shown by the fact that the next day many resented what had happened, and blamed Moses for the death of the rebels. The plague which God sent on the congregation took the lives of many, and Aaron himself became the symbol of deliverance.

7. Sprouting of Aaron's Rod (17:1-13). This story of the rod that budded is rather well known, but its significance can be seen only in the light of the context of the Great Rebellion of Chapter 16. There God gave negative evidence of His choice of Aaron as High Priest, by destroying the other claimants to that honor. He now gives a test which furnishes positive evidence of the same fact.

Moses, at God's command, told the leader of each tribe to bring a rod, representing his tribe. The rod from the tribe of Levi had Aaron's name on it. (It is not clear what was written on the other rods, but probably either the name of the tribe or its leader, or both.) These rods were the leaders' symbols of authority. They were all twelve left overnight in the tabernacle. The next morning the rod of Aaron was seen to have buds, blossoms, and almonds (v. 8). This miracle demonstrated to all the divine approval upon Aaron as high priest. Verses 12-13 express the people's understanding from this that only the authorized priests could come to the Tabernacle with impunity. Thus we see that they had learned their lesson. This final statement is preparation for the instructions of the next chapter.

D. Dues and Duties of Priests and Levites (18:1-32)

This section on the responsibilities and benefits of the Levites and priests is inserted here to emphasize them. It was the priesthood which had been under fire in the great mutiny.

1. Levites' Duties (18:1-7). This is one of the two times when we are told that God gave a message directly to Aaron. The other is in Leviticus 10:8. The instructions here are not really new (cf.

3:1—4:49); but are presented here for clarification. The people seemed to be left in some confusion and fear after the miracle of the budding rod. They were afraid that they would all die, without knowing quite why (17:12-13). Now the message comes directly to Aaron that he and the other priests must *bear the iniquity of the sanctuary*, which means that they themselves, and not the people, are responsible for seeing to it that no one who is not a priest touches what is forbidden to them. They were also responsible to see to it that the Levites do what they are told by the priests, and nothing else (v. 2-3). The priests, and they alone, are responsible for keeping the rules of the tabernacle and seeing that they are kept by others. They are to keep others away from it (v. 5). The Levites are to serve, but they are to serve under the direction and supervision of the priests (vv. 6-7).

2. Priests' Dues (18:8-20). The principle involved in this section is that the priests have not been promised any land in Canaan (v. 20), since they are to be taken up with the work of the Tabernacle and will have no time to farm or make a living otherwise. Since that is true, they are to be taken care of by sharing in the offerings and gifts of the people. Rules are given as to just what is their share. Similar, but slightly different, rules are given in various parts of Leviticus, Deuteronomy, and Ezekiel. Apparently the specific amounts of each offering which belonged to the priests were changed from time to time because of changing circumstances.

Verse 14 speaks of things "devoted" to the Lord, as in Leviticus 27:28. The Hebrew word here is *cherem* (see Appendix on *Holy*), which means more than a mere dedication. It was indicative of a way of devoting a thing to God in such a fashion that it could not be redeemed or ever again used for ordinary purposes. The vow was irrevocable.

The firstborn of all animals belonged to God, but they could be redeemed with a price and used for ordinary purposes. They were *godesh* rather than *cherem*. Both belonged to God, but the first could be redeemed.

The *covenant of salt* (v. 19) apparently means an eternal covenant. (Cf. Lev. 2:13; II Chron. 13:5; Ezek. 43:24; Mark 9:49).

3. Levites' Dues (18:21-24). The Levites, like the priests, are to serve the Tabernacle and be supported by the rest of the Israelites. So the tithes of the other tribes belong to the Levites (v. 24). This is, of course, the background for the oft-quoted scripture in Malachi 3:8-10. If the tithes were not paid, the Levites would be in poverty.

4. Priests' Dues from the Levites (18:25-32). The Levites, in turn, as they received the tithes of the other tribes, must pay a tithe of that to the priests. They paid this just as if what they received was the result of their own agriculture (v. 27). Verses 31-32 must mean that after they have tithed of the tithes which they received, they could freely eat the rest of the tithes. The fact that the tribes had given these tithes to God did not make them untouchable. Note that the instructions of this chapter stress the value of the tithe, and show that no one is exempt from the principle of tithing. Even the Levites paid tithes of the tithes which they received. The tithe is a way of recognizing that all belongs to God. This is a universal principle, and applies to all.

E. Purification from Uncleanness by the Dead (19:1-22)

The rabbis have agreed that there are some things in this chapter that no one understands. One question they asked was why the water which purifies the unclean (vv. 9, 12) makes the person who sprinkles it unclean (vv. 8, 19, 21). They were also puzzled about the significance of the specific materials in verse 6. But if we look away from such details to the ceremony as a whole, we find real values here.

1. Rite of the Red Heifer (19:1-10). The ceremony of the red heifer provides for the removal of defilement resulting from contact with the dead. Death is an aspect of human existence which must not be dodged or put out of mind, but openly faced. The quality of religion is seen in its attitude toward death. The Israelites in the wilderness must have been faced daily with the fact of death. A whole generation died there during that forty years, as another generation grew up to take its place. On occasions, great numbers died at one time from plague. What should be their attitude toward death and the dead? What should they do about burial?

Many of the ideas of the Israelites were the ideas and concepts of the rest of the Near East peoples of that time. In general, they probably thought of death as did some of their pagan neighbors. Yet Israel strongly opposed the funeral rites of pagans (Lev. 19:28; Deut. 14:1-2) as well as attempts to communicate with the dead (Lev. 19:31; 20:6, 27; Deut. 18:11; I Sam. 28:3). Touching a dead person was not sinful, but did render a person unclean for seven days. This meant that he was not qualified for any religious duties (cf. vv. 11-13) during that period. Uncleanness was not sinful, though it was in some ways treated like sin (cf. Appendix on *Holy*). Uncleanness had to be cleansed. That is the purpose of this rite of the red heifer (v. 9).

Note the number of different people involved in this ceremony. The heifer is in some sense given by the whole people (v. 2), and many individuals are involved in the different parts of the ceremony. The heifer is killed for the cleansing of the whole people, and the whole people were involved in the preparation. Briefly summarized, the rite was this: A specially chosen red heifer (v. 2) was killed outside the camp (v. 3), and the whole was burnt (v. 5) along with cedar, hyssop, and scarlet (v. 6). Then clean water was mixed with the ashes (v. 17) and used for sprinkling on persons and things which were unclean (vv. 9, 19).

This chapter is unique in specifying the color of the animal to be sacrificed (v. 2), and no reason is obvious (could it symbolize blood?). There is the usual emphasis on the requirement that the animal be without certain defects (cf. Lev. 22:22-24 for a list). It must never have been used for ordinary purposes (*upon which never came yoke*).

This is the only animal which was required to be killed outside the camp (v. 3). So this is apparently what the author of Hebrews was referring to when he compared it to Jesus, who died outside the city (Heb. 13:11-12).

It is hard to say why all the people who take active part in the ceremony are thereby rendered unclean for the rest of the day. At the least we can see that this emphasizes the powerfulness of the rite. The water for impurity is not to be carelessly handled. God had ordained all of this, and one must be careful in the presence of God's cleansing power.

2. General Procedure for Cleansing (19:11-13). The one who touched a dead body was unclean for seven days (v. 11). As a matter of fact, this was a good health rule, at least in the case of those who died from contagious diseases. More importantly, it precluded such pagan practices as worship of the dead, spiritism, and black magic.

The person who was unclean had to cause himself to be purified with the water on the third and seventh day, or he must be cut off from the people. The water was to be thrown on him.

3. Specific Rules of Cleansing (vv. 14-22). Verses 14-15 show that when a person died in a tent, all the people in the tent, and all the things in the tent were to be treated as unclean for seven days. But if the body was in the open, actual contact with the body was necessary to render a person unclean (v. 16).

Note that on the seventh day, the person was to cleanse himself again, and also wash himself and his clothes (v. 19). So the cleansing was not only ceremonial, but physical. This was a good health rule. But it was more than that. In all of this concept of uncleanness after touching the dead, there is involved the close relationship between sin and death. The individual's death is not the result of his sin, but being subject to death is part of the penalty of sin (Gen. 3:19b, 22). So death partakes of the curse of sin.

On a particular Sabbath each year, Jews read this chapter and Ezekiel 36:16-28, to emphasize the necessity of cleanness in order to keep the Passover. Such passages helped to teach Israel that it is God who sets the requirements for approach to Him. It is only God who can make man acceptable to Him. Man cannot approach God on his own human terms and conditions. If man is rendered unfit for approach to God, only God Himself is able to provide the cleansing he needs. No wonder the author of Hebrews felt the analogy between the red heifer and Jesus (Heb. 13:11-12).

IV. MARCH FROM KADESH TO MOAB (20:1—22:1)

The fourteenth chapter told of the condemnation to forty years of wandering in the wilderness (a round number for nearly thirty-eight years). This chapter tells of events in the last of those years. Chapters 15 to 19 record only two historical events — the revolt of Korah and the man who picked up wood on the sabbath — and neither of them is dated in any way. So this period of wandering is a gap in the history.

It is not hard to see why the wandering in the wilderness is passed over in silence. The rebellious people who took part in this period had forfeited all right to the redemptive plan of God. They actually had no part in the plan which God had been carrying out, and continued to carry out through their children. The story of what they did in the wilderness was not part of the redemptive story, since it was only the story of condemned men wandering until they died.

So it is that the story which was interrupted at the end of Chapter 14 is resumed at this point. We are told of the death of Miriam and then of Aaron, showing that they did not enter the promised land. We are also told of some of the final events of the forty years.

A. Sojourn at Kadesh (20:1-21)

The Israelites were at Kadesh when they were told to begin their wandering by going towards the Red Sea (13:26). Now they are at Kadesh again, and we are given no clue as to where they had been in the meantime. They may have traveled far. Or they may have milled around in the area of Kadesh. Some feel that they may have scattered out during that time, since there are indications that they did not keep up all of the annual ceremonies.

1. Miriam's Death (20:1). Although some scholars place this much earlier, it cannot be proven wrong to consider this the first month of the last year of wandering. This year was then the fortieth since they had left Egypt, and the thirty-eighth of their wandering. They are back at Kadesh-Barnea, at the northern boundary of the wilderness of Paran and the southern boundary of the desert of Zin. Once more they were near the promised land. This time they would actually enter it, but not by the southern route. They would skirt around Moab and enter by crossing the

Jordan. This meant a longer journey, but it also made possible a more effective conquest.

It was here, at the end of the wandering, that Miriam died. Like her two brothers, Moses and Aaron, she failed to enter the promised land. In spite of her sins, however, she had won a place for herself as a good leader of the people. In some measure she made up for earlier failures by later faithfulness. Surely this can offer us encouragement.

Yet it is interesting and instructive to note that, though Miriam was one of the three most important leaders of this period, her death and burial is told in five Hebrew words (eight in English). The work of God is greater than any of the individuals who participate in it. When individuals die, God's work goes on.

2. Miracle at Meribah (20:2-13). The event here described is quite similar to that in Exodus 17:1-7, which is placed forty years earlier, and far to the southwest, at Massah. In both cases, the location was accordingly known as *Meribah* ("striving"). These have been called two versions of the same event, but we need to see that our text describes two similar rebellions of two successive generations. Each generation must make its own mistakes and learn its own lessons. We seldom learn from our parents all that we really ought to know!

So once again the people complain rebelliously (vv. 3-5), and this time Moses loses patience completely with the pettishness they showed. He was a great man, and the Bible does not hesitate to say so. But he was human, and sinned, and the Bible does not hesitate to say that also! He sinned in such a way that God refused to let him enter the promised land (v. 12), although he was allowed to see it (cf. 27:12-14).

Verses 3-6 set the stage for the miracle and the sin, by describing the murmuring of the people because of the lack of water. The people so far forgot their blessings as to say that they would be better off dead. This is just like the complaints of their parents so long before (Exod. 17:3-4). They still asked in the same way why they were not allowed to stay in Egypt. They simply refused to face the future with any hope or trust in God.

The complaints of verse 5 were surely uncalled for. They knew that this was a temporary stopping place, and that they could not expect to find gardens, vineyards, or farms here. But once they began their complaint about water, they childishly complained about many other things. We can suppose also that they were remembering how their parents had been at this very same place so long before, and found there their bitter disappointment. Possibly this memory added to their distress. Their parents had gotten this far and had turned back. Would they be able to go on?

We cannot overlook the pathos of verse 6. Moses and Aaron had surely been tried during these long years in the Sinai Peninsula, and now they were at the breaking point. And in spite of all the great aspects of Moses' character, he did have a breaking point. He came to the point where he sinned against God grievously.

There has been much discussion as to the exact nature of Moses' sin. The fact is that in most of what he did, he was following the directions of the Lord explicitly. Verses 7-11 tell of the command of the Lord, and of Moses' actions. What was his sin? Some commentators (e.g., Clarke, Hanke) have felt that his sin lay in his striking the rock, rather than speaking to it. But was this slight deviation from procedure the great sin of his lifetime?

Moses spoke very sharply to the people about their rebellious attitude (v. 10), Surely they deserved it. They needed to have someone tell them how wrong they were. But was this also his great sin?

Such scholars as Gray, McNeile, and Noth have long insisted that part of the story is lost, and that there is no way now to know what Moses did that was so wrong. Some redactor or copyist, they feel, dropped that part of the story from the record, perhaps in order to protect the memory of Moses.

But an answer is possible. A comparison of verse 12 with 27:14 shows that God is accusing Moses of failing "to sanctify me" in the eyes of the children of Israel. When Moses prepared to strike the rock, he exclaimed, "Must *we* fetch you water. . ."? Moses went too far in suggesting that he himself was being ordered to perform a miracle. Instead of doing it all in the name of the Lord, Moses acted as if he were doing this in his own might. He did not clearly act and speak so as to give all the glory to God, and magnify the power of God in the eyes of the people. He took to himself the glory which belongs to God alone, and this is close to blasphemy. If the people were really to be the people of God, they must constantly recognize that they were under *divine* leadership. And Moses must know that he is leader *under God*. Failing to demonstrate that fact before the people would be fatal to his leadership.

So God told Moses that he would not be able to enter the land of promise, nor to lead the people all the way into it. But the fact that God did give the people water is proof that God may perform miracles even though the one who prays is not fully approved by God. The people received the water they needed, but Moses was not blessed for his part in the matter. On the contrary, he was punished for his actions — the very actions through which the water was supplied! God honored the need of the people and gave them the water, in spite of Moses' failure. (For another illustration of the way in which God did good things for the people "for His name's sake" rather than for their goodness' sake, see Ezekiel 36:21-24.) An answer to prayer is not necessarily proof that a person is approved by God.

3. Israel and Edom (20:14-21). Since the Israelites had tried and failed to enter Canaan directly from Kadesh, they now decided to enter from the east, from across the Jordan. The shortest way to get to that entrance was to go east and north through Edom, on whose border they now were. So Moses sent messengers to the king of Edom with a conciliatory message. They told the king of their history, explained their peaceful intentions, and asked to be allowed to cross the country, promising to stick to the main trade route and to pay for any water or crops they needed. The king refused (v. 18), and even after they explained further how they would pay for any damage done (v. 19), the king still threatened war, and actually sent men out to fight Israel (v. 20).

The result of this incident was that the Israelites went southeast to the head of the Gulf of Aqabah, then northeast and north around Edom to the Arnon River, then west to the Jordan. Thus their journey was much longer than it would have been if the Edomites had been more friendly.

Several points in this passage merit remark. For one thing, the whole passage is marked by the characteristically Semitic idiom of speaking of a whole nation as though it were one person, and switching back and forth from plural to singular and back to plural. This is common in Hebrew, but seems strange to English readers. Second, note the reference to the "angel" in verse 16. Both here and in Exodus 23:20, the angel could be Moses, for the same Hebrew word means both "angel" and "messenger." The situation is more complex in Exodus 32:34, but might still be Moses, since he was sent by God. The expression is characteristic of the E material. A third matter here is the looseness with which the Old Testament uses the word *city* (v. 16) to mean any place where people live. The "highway" (vv. 17, 19) must not be thought of as anything more than a path, as true highways were not known before Roman times. This was probably the caravan route between Egypt and Transjordan countries. No doubt Moses felt sure he would be able to use it, since so many others did.

B. En route for Moab (20:22–22:1)

1. Aaron's Death (20:22-29). All we really know about the location of Mount Hor, is that it was in the edge of Edom, near the border (cf. 33:37). The traditional site, near Petra, could not fit this statement, since it is in the midst of Edom. Recently a site north of Kadesh has been suggested, called Jebel Madurah. Wherever it was, there Aaron died. God told Aaron and Moses that Aaron would not enter the land because of the incident at Meribah (v. 24; cf. v. 12). Verses 25-28 tell of the dignified death of Aaron, and the installation of his son Eleazer as high priest by putting on him the robes of office. The people then mourned for Aaron thirty days. He was a great man, in spite of his failures.

2. Defeat and Victory at Hormah (21:1-3). The simplest way to deal with these three verses is to say that we do not know what they are talking about. We do not know where or when the battle in verse 1 was fought, as there are serious problems with all the suggested solutions. We do not know when the destruction of verse 3 took place. The passage seems to describe a single incident, yet it is a summary of the whole of the "conquest" of Joshua. And Hormah ("doomed to destruction") is the collective name which could be applied to every city the Israelites destroyed in Canaan. Herein lies the meaning of the passage, all those who utterly resist God are to be utterly destroyed. The Hebrew word *cherem*, from which *Hormah* is derived, means "devoted" to a god other than the Lord, and therefore of destruction. Although we reject the way the Israelites took the destruction into their own hands, the ancient concept of *cherem* gives meaning to the New Testament teaching about hell — the final destruction of those who utterly oppose God.

3. The Bronze Serpent (21:4-9). Being forbidden to pass through Edom (20:14-21), the Israelites turned southeast toward the eastern arm of the Red Sea (v. 4a), which is now called the Gulf of Aqabah. They had been very close to the southern part of Canaan, and were now traveling away from it, through very desolate country. No wonder they were discouraged and impatient (v. 4b). This country is very desolate, and in the summer is extremely hot and miserable.

Once more the people are complaining that they have been brought out of the land of Egypt only to die of starvation. It was not that they did not have anything to eat, for God was supplying manna every day. But their imagination made them feel that the food they had eaten in Egypt was far better than the manna, which they called "light" in value, or "worthless." They were "making light of" the very gift of God which had kept them alive all this time. They were sick of manna, figuratively speaking, in a childish sort of way.

This kind of complaining had usually led to God performing a miracle to give the people what they wanted, but this time it led to punishment. This time the punishment came in the form of serpents whose bite caused burning pain and inflammation. Many died after being bitten. (Since the Hebrew word for *fiery* is *seraphim*, some have seen some connection with Isaiah 6:2, and with the serapis cult of Egypt of a much later period. Etymological evidence is against the former connection, and the date is against the latter.)

When the people began to lose their loved ones, and became afraid of dying themselves, they began to repent of their sin. In response to the prayer of Moses, God gave a plan for healing. He had sent the punishment but was quick to forgive. Moses was to make a brass replica of one of the serpents and put it on a post in the midst of the camp. Then anyone who was bitten was to look at the brass serpent, and he would be healed, and would not die.

We are clearly told that the healing power was not in the brass serpent itself, but in the fact that God had ordered the whole process. When they looked at the serpent, they looked in obedience to God, who had ordered it to be made, and who commanded the looking. God was willing to forgive and heal, but He wanted the people to know that forgiveness is not a casual act. They must do more than merely say they were sorry and ask for forgiveness. Then God Himself did the healing, in response to repentance and forgiveness.

This story is very familiar to Christians, because of the way Jesus used the brass serpent to illustrate the fact that when He Himself would be lifted up (on a cross), He would bring healing to the world, as individuals looked to Him (John 3:14-15). The brass serpent was not necessarily a Messianic prediction or type, but it is easy to see how Jesus could find it a fitting illustration of this aspect of Himself. There is therefore no need to seek for meanings in the details.

The brass serpent was preserved until the time of Hezekiah, who destroyed it because it had become an object of worship, which was idolatry (II Kings 18:4). This whole incident is also mentioned by Paul (I Cor. 10:9).

4. On the March (21:10-20). These verses tell very quickly of the long, hard march all the rest of the way around the south and east of Edom to the Arnon, and then west. We do not know the exact location of any of these places, though we can guess at the approximate places. We do know the Arnon, which flows west into about the center of the Dead Sea. It meanders through the bottom of a deep trench like a miniature Grand Canyon — up to seventeen hundred feet deep. This branches out at the end into four branches. On the whole, this made a formidable barrier to their progress and therefore made quite an impression on the Israelites.

Since we cannot identify the places mentioned, we can learn only a little from these verses, but that little is interesting. Two scraps of poems are quoted (vv. 14b-15; 17b-18). The first is said to be in the Book of the Wars of the Lord, a book which is otherwise totally unknown to us. The fact that the Old Testament refers to several such books, and that some of them were written very early, shows that there was no lack of writing among the Israelites from the time of Moses onward. References such as these must not be ignored in any discussion of the authorship of the Pentateuch. The second poem is part of an ancient folk song.

Pisgah and Nebo are high hills just east of the Jordan not far from the northern end of the Dead Sea. From them one can get the same breathtaking view Moses had of the land from the Dead Sea to the mountains of Samaria.

5. Defeat of the Amorites (21:21-32). This passage tells of the victory over Sihon, king of the Amorites. This victory and the one over Og (vv. 33-35) were the last two before entrance to the land of Canaan, and made a deep impression on the Israelites for that reason. The story is also told in Deuteronomy 2:24-37 and Judges 11:19-22, and is referred to in Deuteronomy 31:4; Joshua 2:10; 9:10; 12:5; 13:27; I Kings 4:19; Psalm 135:11; 136:19. Nevertheless, the story is very sketchily told, and leaves questions unanswered.

In verse 21 the Israelites are apparently in the position described in verse 13, at the River Arnon, the border between Moab and the Amorite territory. Sihon, according to verse 24, held territory bounded on the south by the Arnon, on the north by the Jabbok, and on the east by the border of the Ammonites. The western border was the Jordan and Dead Sea. Israel sent messengers to Sihon, as they had previously to the king of Edom, asking permission to cross his land. Sihon refused permission, and brought an army out against Israel. We are not told why the Israelites reacted differently than they had at Edom, but instead of seeking to go around, they went forth with their army to meet Sihon, and defeated him. So Israel took the cities of Sihon (v. 25), which are not named except for Heshbon, the capital. As verse 26 tells us, Sihon had only recently wrested this territory from the king of Moab, whose territory had extended farther north.

Verses 27-30 quote a ballad, which is difficult to interpret, partly because of allusions which are obscure, and partly because we cannot know the original setting of the ballad. But the jubilation of the whole passage, and the many other allusions to it in the Old Testament, show the strength of the impression this victory made on the Israelites. They had just come through the discouragement of a long hard march through inhospitable and miserable territory. They and their parents had spent their lives desiring to get to the land of promise, and now this victory put them on the very verge of crossing over into the land at last. Now they could feel that God was really on their side, and would give them what He had promised so long before.

Note what a change one victory can make in the disposition and outlook of a people or a person. Years of discouragement and depression can be blotted from memory by the change of viewpoint brought about by a victory. So why be discouraged? "If God is for us, who is against us?" (Rom. 8:31b RSV).

6. Defeat of Og (21:33-35). These three verses tell of another victory which encouraged the Israelites. After defeating Sihon, they pressed on northward into Bashan, the district east of the Sea of Galilee, and there they met Og, king of Bashan, in battle at Edrei, his capital city. This city is northeast of Ramoth-Gilead. Og was a giant of a man (Deut. 3:11), and ruled over a very fertile land. This victory over Og is also told in almost the same words in Deuteronomy 3:1-3, and further elaborated in verses 4-11 of that chapter. There we are told that the Israelites took every one of his walled and fortified cities. How long this took we are not told, but it means that the Israelites must have stayed for some time east of the Jordan.

There are archeological indications that Bashan, the land of Sihon, Moab, and Edom were all established shortly before the coming of the Israelites. In this whole area, the people had within a very short time given up the nomadic life and built cities. Some of the cities which the Israelites took were still in the process of being built and fortified. (The Philistines were at the same time migrating to the southern Mediterranean seacoast.)

We are told in verse 34 that God promised victory over Og. We are not told that they had any such command or promise concerning the battle with Sihon (vv. 21-32).

7. Encampment Opposite Jericho (22:1). After the two victories over Sihon and Og, which gave them control of the whole area east of the Jordan, the Israelites finally camped just east of the Jordan River opposite Jericho. Now they were at the edge of the promised land and, with important victories behind them, they felt ready to enter at last.

V. THE STORY OF BALAAM (22:2–24:25)

A. Balak and Balaam (22:2-40)

There is no way to know how this section came to be a part of the Biblical record. No Israelites were present at the events recorded. How could they have learned these things from their enemies? But the fact is that the story is here, and many of the details fit what we know of Mesopotamian life of that period. We know from the records at Mari that there were "prophets" like Balaam in Mesopotamia, who could be hired to handle a specific problem or trouble. The oracles of Balaam are full of parallels to Ugaritic literature of the period.

The real theme of the Book of Balaam, as these chapters were called in the Talmud, is apt to be lost in speculation about details. Though we cannot know where the Israelites got the story, we can see that they told the story to show that God was on the side of His people, Israel, and could even work through pagans for their good and protection. So it is that Balak and Balaam, interesting as they are, are not the main interest here. The real characters or antagonists in the story are Israel and Moab. And the chief point is that God worked for the good of His people. God's power in behalf of His people was exerted beyond their boundaries. Yahweh is thus portrayed as more than a tribal god; He is the God of the nations, with real power and authority over all of them. Balaam stooped to do what no Hebrew prophet would ever do. He sold his services as a prophet. Yet God found a way to speak to and through even him!

For this reason, we do not have to puzzle over the correct assessment of Balaam's character. The older commentators agreed in calling him the embodiment of evil, but in the last centuries there have been those who have thought of him as a very good man. The fact is that, like many others, he was a mixture of both good and evil. We do not have to decide which predominated, and to what extent. The main thing is that God used him for the good of Israel, and spoke through him prophecies of good things to come for the Israelites. From the viewpoint of this one great fact, all of the puzzling features of the story, including the talking animal, are all subsidiary elements.

1. Moab's Fear of Israel (22:2-4). In view of the recent victories of Israel over Sihon and Og, the fear of the king of Moab is natural and realistic. The Israelites had shown no animosity

towards Moab, but they had conquered all the territory to the far north of them, so it is not surprising that the Moabites were afraid.

The *elders of Midian* (v. 4) are mentioned again in verse 7, but play no further part in the story, and it is hard to see why they are mentioned at all. The duplications or repetitions in verse 3 and some other puzzling features are solved by form critics by their concept of the interweaving of two stories (J and E), but since such details have little or no effect on the major point of the story, and since they leave the problems unsolved in any case, they can be ignored in our study. Some of the problems are no doubt traceable to the totally unknown way in which the Israelites got hold of the story in the first place.

2. Balak's First Embassy (22:5-14). Balak, king of Moab, decided to try to get help against the Israelites, of whom he was so much afraid. He sent for Balaam, who was some sort of prophet. Though a pagan, Balaam knew something of Yahweh and tried to serve Him. How much he knew, it is impossible to say. He is said to be from Pethor, which is commonly identified as Pitru, just south of Carchemish, four hundred miles north of Moab. (On very precarious grounds, some have so reconstructed the text as to suggest that Balaam was from Edom or Ammon, very near to Moab. The evidence is against this.)

What Balak wanted was for Balaam to pronounce a curse against the Israelites. In almost all the ancient Near Eastern countries, there was strong belief in the power of words to help or to hurt people. A blessing or a curse had real power to help or to destroy, and especially so if it were pronounced in the sight of the person, and by one who had more than usual effectiveness in such blessing or cursing. So the message Balak sends to Balaam asks him to come pronounce such a curse on Israel (v. 6). He sent messengers with the message, and with money or goods with which to hire Balaam to do the job (v. 7).

Balaam seems to be inclined to go with the messengers, but did tell them that they would have to wait for him to get Yahweh's approval (v. 8). This fact is puzzling only if one is determined to think of Balaam as all good or bad. On the contrary, he is presented as a pagan who knew something of Yahweh, and through whom Yahweh spoke – in spite of the flaws in his character.

Balaam expected to hear from God and God did come to him, perhaps in a dream, and told him not to go with the men, nor to curse Israel (vv. 10, 12). Accordingly, he was obedient enough to tell Balak's messengers that he would not go with them, as Yahweh had forbidden it (v. 13). So the messengers returned to Balak without Balaam but did not relay the reason he did not return with them.

3. Balak's Second Embassy (22:15-21). Balak was not willing to take no for an answer. Assuming that he had not offered a large enough gift, he sent more important messengers with a larger gift or price, begging Balaam to come curse the people (vv. 15-17). There is no indication that Balaam felt any such attitudes. There is, in fact, just the opposite indication in the reply he gives (v. 18). This stirring reply is worthy of any man of God, and is a credit to Balaam no matter what other flaws there may have been in his character. He declared positively that he would not go beyond the command of Yahweh his God, no matter what the king might offer him.

Yet Balaam did tell the men they could spend the night, and that if he got any further word from the Lord he would obey it (v. 19). Instead of trying to read more into verse 19 than is clearly said, we can assume that he meant what he said in verse 18. He would do no more nor less that God told him to do, and would continue to wait on the Lord for instructions. (The significance of God's message in v. 20 would be more clear if we read "since" instead of the "if" of KJV.) Since Balaam had declared so positively that he would obey God implicitly, God told him he could go with the men, but warned him that he must do exactly as he was told, and as he had promised. So he saddled up the next morning and started off.

4. Balaam and His Ass (22:22-35). This small section is full of puzzles, if not inconsistencies. The speaking ass is only one of these. God had told Balaam to go (v. 20), but is angry with him for going (v. 22). He and the messengers started off together (v. 21), but in verses 22-34 he is apparently alone. Not only are we told that the ass spoke (v. 28), but even more surprising is the calm way in which Balaam answered, as though this were common (v. 29). In verse 29 he is wishing he had a sword with which to kill the ass, he is so angry, yet he is calmly convinced by the argument of the ass (v. 30).

Maimonides made the attractive suggestion that verses 22-34 took place in a dream or dream-vision which Balaam had during the night. This would answer all the questions about the passage, without denying the possibility of miracle, but would leave us wondering why we are not told it was all a dream. It is told as simple fact, though not *sober* fact, for the humor in the whole story is apparent. And whether Balaam was asleep or awake, the resulting message is the same. God wanted to impress on Balaam that he must say only what he is told to say, nothing more and nothing less. In any case, it is easy to understand why God would have to use unusual means to get His will done by such a man as Balaam.

The anger of God (v. 22) is best explained by assuming that Balaam, in spite of his strong declaration in verse 18, was being tempted in his heart to somehow please Balak so as to obtain the promised reward. Only God could know how close he might have been to yielding to this temptation.

The *angel of the Lord* (v. 22) was an angel of mercy, sent by God to keep Balaam from doing wrong. But, as so often happens, what God meant for good was considered troublesome interference. It would be a good thing if all of us could have the right kind of interference at the right time to keep us from doing wrong! Balaam did not understand what was going on, and tried to get the ass to continue on the journey he had determined to make (v. 23). He would have been better off if he could have understood earlier.

Finally the angel got the ass to stop completely and lie down and refuse to get up and go on! This was the last straw. Balaam could be patient no longer, and beat the ass with a staff he carried. He was evidently not a cruel man, or he would have beaten it before, but now his patience was gone.

What looked bad for Balaam was really for his good! How often this is true in our own experiences, but we know it not until later. Then we look back on the experience, and see that we did not understand what was really going on! If we could only learn to see God's will more clearly and more quickly, we could save ourselves much trouble. God finds it hard to catch our attention.

When the angel finally got the attention of Balaam (v. 31), the prophet was easily persuaded to do right. It was not so much that he was stubborn as that he had his mind so set on one plan of action that he could not think of anything else. When the angel states that the way of Balaam is displeasing to God (v. 32), he apparently means that Balaam's mind was so taken up with the temptation of the gold that he was in real danger of yielding. Balaam quickly repented, and offered to go back home immediately (v. 34). At this point, the angel told Balaam to go on with the men, but warned him again to say only God's words.

We should pray for such a tender conscience that it will take much less than a speaking animal to turn us away from temptation!

5. Balaam's Visit with Balak (22:36-40). Both here and in the rest of the story we see the sharp contrast between the attitudes of Balak and Balaam. Balak wants only to see his enemies effectively cursed, and assumes that the money and honor he can offer

will purchase this. Balaam, thoroughly chastened by all that has happened, wants only to say what Yahweh tells him.

Apparently messengers sent word to Balak that the long-awaited Balaam was actually arriving, and Balak prepared a royal welcome, probably at Ar (cf. 21:15). This was at the Arnon River, which was the boundary of Balak's land (v. 36). Balak chides Balaam for not coming at the first call, still assuming that Balaam only waited for a larger reward (v. 37). Balaam shows a far different spirit when he replies that he is here, but that he can say only what the Lord commands him to say, since he has no power of his own to bless or to curse (v. 38). This is quite a thing to hear from a pagan fortune-teller, but it is an indication that Balaam had some real knowledge of the Lord. This is only one of the many indications in the Old Testament that God did not limit His work to the people of Israel, but spoke to anyone who would listen. Balak apparently did not take his words seriously.

We do not know the location of Kirjath-huzoth (v. 39), where the sacrifice was made, nor are we given any explanation of the sacrifice. This may have been merely a way of extending hospitality.

B. Balaam's Oracles (22:41—24:25)

The rest of the story is the record of the way in which Balaam makes four poetic pronouncements over the camp of Israel. This is what he was brought here to do, but the pronouncements are not of the kind for which Balak was willing to pay. They are not curses, as he wanted, but blessings.

In this section we see that Balaam went about his work more like a Mesopotamian diviner than a Hebrew prophet, even though he acknowledged the Lord. He offered no objection to Balak's worship of Baal, yet he insisted on saying only the words of Yahweh.

Four times Balaam declared the word of the Lord, even though to do so meant that he would not receive the rich reward offered by Balak. Each time Balak took him to a different place and offered him another chance to curse Israel. After the third time, he told Balaam he might as well quit and go home, if he was not going to curse Israel. Then Balaam delivered his fourth message, in which he not only blessed Israel, but pronounced the doom of Moab.

1. First Oracle (22:41—23:12). The day after Balaam's arrival, Balak took him to a local sanctuary of Baal, which, as usual was on a high place (v. 41). From there they could see one end

of the camp of Israel. We assume that the rest of the large camp was hidden by the hills.

As was noted above, Balaam went about his preparations like a Mesopotamian fortune-teller. Something of purely pagan divination is seen in the way he prepares to give the message of the Lord. Similar records of the work of pagan diviners of the future are found in inscriptions from Mari. But the point of the record is that in spite of all this, Balaam was led by the power of Yahweh to proclaim just what He desired.

When they get to the high place, Balaam takes charge and orders seven altars to be built for the offering of *seven oxen and seven rams* (23:1). Then Balaam ordered Balak to stay by the altars while he went off to get a message from the Lord. Yahweh did speak to him and gave him a message to declare to Balak (v. 5), so he went back to Balak and his chief men who were all eagerly waiting for the curse.

Verses 7-10 are the message which Yahweh gave Balaam. "Oracle" is probably a much better translation of the Hebrew *mashal* than "parable." The oracle is in the form of a poem, and is unmitigated praise of Israel. It is the exact opposite of the curse for which Balak was willing to pay. Balaam closes with the exclamation of hope that he might share in their fate.

Naturally this sort of message disturbed Balak deeply. He is amazed that Balaam could so speak when he was hired to do the opposite (v. 11). But Balaam calmly replies that he can do nothing but what Yahweh commands him to do. His answer would do justice to any Hebrew prophet (v. 12).

2. Second Oracle (23:13-26). Balak then suggested that they go to another hill where they could see the camp of Israel, and try again to get the kind of message Balak wanted. Balaam did not encourage him in this, and there is no indication that Balaam expected Yahweh to change His mind, but he did not refuse to try again.

So they went together to a place at the top of Pisgah (v. 14), which cannot be located certainly since Pisgah is the name of a range of heights, rather than a particular mountain. They offered there another fourteen animals on seven more altars. Again Balaam left Balak to stand by the altars while he went to consult Yahweh (v. 15). When he returned, Balak impatiently asked for the message (v. 17).

The oracle is again a poem (vv. 18-24), this time a little stronger. The oracle begins by directly addressing Balak and telling him he is wrong to think that God is like man who can change his mind. God had given a blessing through Balaam, and cannot recall it (v. 20). The blessing is irrevocable.

Verse 21a speaks of the nation of Israel in ideal terms as a sinless nation; it is true that Israel had not so completely turned from God to idols that God could not lead them any more. The latter part of the verse declares that God dwells in their midst. God brought them from Egypt and has great strength (v. 22), so that there is no way for anything to hurt them. Verse 23a may be an elaboration of verse 21a, saying that divination is not used by the Israelites, or it may be saying that no enchantment or curse can have any effect on Israel. In any case, verses 23b and 24 give a clear picture of the strength of Israel for conquest.

At this point, it is not hard to understand the desperation of Balak. He tells Balaam that if he cannot curse Israel, he had better not say anything at all (v. 25). But Balaam simply reminds him that he had told him before that he would have to say whatever the Lord commanded (v. 26).

3. Third Oracle (23:27—24:13). It had appeared that Balak was ready to give up and send Balaam home (v. 25), but he decided to try again. So now they went to the top of Peor, and went through the same process as before (vv. 28-30).

Here we have something different. After the sacrifices were made, Balaam did not go off as before to learn the message of the Lord (24:1). He did not try to get any different message from the Lord; he was sure now that God would again bless Israel through him. So he looked off toward the camp of Israel "and the spirit of God came upon him" (v. 2). Verses 3b and 4b imply that he fell into some sort of trance, though this is not certain. Both the translation and the interpretation of verses 3-4 are obscure. All that is sure about them is that Balaam was claiming divine inspiration of this oracle. This record of the inspiration of Balaam is another indication of the kind of universalism which is in the Old Testament but is so often overlooked. The Hebrews did not limit the work of God to themselves.

As Balaam saw the orderly camp of Israel, he compared the people of God to the Garden of Eden, planted by God himself, and fertile (vv. 6-7). Again he declares that it was God who brought them out of Egypt (v. 8; cf. 23:22), and who will make them prevail against their enemies. Israel is like a lion, whom no one has courage to disturb. He concludes with a simple blessing on Israel (v. 9b).

This third oracle was so disturbing to Balak that he slapped his hands together in desperation and berated Balaam for blessing Israel three times when he had been called to curse them (v. 10).

So he is through with Balaam. He tells him what he has passed up by obeying God. He had missed a rich reward because of his God. Balaam calmly reminds Balak that he had originally told his messengers that no amount of silver or gold would cause him to say anything but what Yahweh told him to say (vv. 12-13).

4. Farewell Oracle (24:14-25). Balaam says that he will go home, but first he will inform (KJV has "advertise") Balak of the future fate of Moab, and does not wait for Balak to ask for the oracle (v. 14).

Once more we have words which may suggest a trance, but may mean something else entirely (vv. 15-17). (The word *trance* is not in the Hebrew). What is again clear is that Balaam is claiming divine inspiration. Much in this oracle is obscure because we do not know the significance of some of the names used. But the message clearly predicts the downfall of many nations, beginning with Moab (v. 17b). Moab fell to Israel during the reign of David (II Sam. 8:2).

Then Balaam left for home (v. 25). Since he was killed among the Midianites shortly afterwards (31:8), we can suppose that on the way home he stopped with them and met his end.

VI. MISCELLANEOUS LAWS AND INCIDENTS
   (25:1–32:42)

A. Physical and Spiritual Wantonness (25:1-18)

The Israelites continually found it difficult to keep away from the women and the gods of their heathen neighbors. These two incidents are samples of what happened to them when they yielded to these two temptations.

1. Wantonness with Moab (25:1-5). Israel was encamped at Shittim, their last camp before entering Canaan proper. They had conquered most of the territory east of the Jordan and were now camped on the border of Moab, against which they had no military intentions. But now they not only committed adultery with Moabite women (v. 1), but they committed spiritual adultery by worshiping Moabite gods (v. 2). Moses took swift action and ordered the sinners to be hanged publicly (vv. 4-5).

If it were not for 31:16 and Revelation 2:14, we would not know that it was Balaam who was involved in these two incidents. He apparently induced the Moabites and Midianites to send their women to entice the Israelites into idolatry. What could have been in his mind we do not know. Was he still trying to find a way to earn the gold of Balak? If so, his death among the Midianites (31:8) was fitting punishment.

2. Wantonness with Midian (25:6-18). Apparently this incident (vv. 6, 8) was only one example of wicked adultery with Midianite women which brought a terrible plague on the camp as punishment (vv. 8b, 9). This plague is apparently the cause of the weeping of remorse and repentance (v. 6b). But at least one man was not weeping (v. 6a), and was quickly executed for his brazenness (vv. 7-8). (The word translated "tent" in KJV is only used here in the Old Testament, and is of unknown meaning.) So the plague was stopped, but only after the camp was decimated. Phinehas, whose action brought the sinning and the plague to an end, was given a promise that he and his descendants would be priests forever (vv. 10-13).

God's command to fight against the Midianites for their tempting Israel to idolatry (vv. 16-18) was obeyed and this episode is recorded in Chapter 31.

B. Second Census (26:1-65)

It had been nearly forty years since the last census had been taken (chap. 1), and now the people were about to go into the land of promise. There the land would be divided among them, and it was important to know how many there were in each tribe. Besides that, there had just been another disastrous plague among them (25:8-9) and some of the tribes were depleted. So God commanded another census (v. 2).

The figures resulting from the census are given in verses 5-51, except for the count of the Levites, which is again given separately (vv. 57-62). The figures given here are comparable with those in Chapter 1. (See the discussion on page 18 for an explanation of the totals.) Some tribes had increased, while Simeon had decreased, but the total for all the tribes is about the same as before.

Verses 52-56 explain that in the land of Canaan, the land will be divided by lot among the tribes, according to their population. The concluding statement (vv. 63-65) says that God's word had been fulfilled, and that only Joshua and Caleb remain of the former generation. All those over twenty in the first census had died in the wilderness.

C. Law of Female Inheritance (27:1-11)

After the census, and the explanation of the way in which the land would be divided among the men counted in each tribe, a legal problem was posed by the daughters of a man who died without sons (vv. 1-4). Since there was no law specifically covering such a case, these women wanted the matter cleared up, and so brought the matter through proper channels to Moses. Moses not only decided in favor of the women, but laid down a new and general principle that would cover such cases in the future (vv. 6-11). This rule was an important step for women among the Jews.

D. Appointment of Joshua (27:12-23)

God tells Moses (vv. 12-14) to go up into a high mountain where he can look at the land of promise before he dies. He is reminded that he cannot enter the land with the people because of his sin at Meribah (cf. chap. 20). This command to Moses is repeated in Deuteronomy 32: 48-52; and its fulfillment is described in Deuteronomy 34:1-7, after the delivery of the sermons which make up most of that Book. There was much yet to do, but God warns Moses now that his time is almost up, and that he must leave the conquest to another man. This must have been a deep disappointment to Moses, but he faced it as a man should.

Mount Abarim is one of the peaks of Mount Nebo, which is

ten or fifteen miles east of the northern end of the Dead Sea. Here Moses would be able to look across the deep canyon of the Jordan River and the Dead Sea to the high plateau and mountains on the other side. From this mountain he could see how near the people now were to the land God had promised, and see that his work had not been in vain. He could also see the difficult route the people would have to take to get down to the Jordan and up into the hills on the other side.

Notice that although Moses had sinned, and was being punished, God yet spoke to him. This means that God had forgiven him, and now accepted him as a godly man in spite of his past sin. This is a clear indication to us that God's forgiveness of our sin does not take away all the results of sin. Many sins carry with them results which are life-long. One can never be, after sin, exactly what he could have been if he had never committed the sin. Even though God forgives the sin, and cleanses the heart, the fact of the sin is not erased from history.

Moses knew the importance of the right successor in this place of leadership, and asked God, who knows the hearts of men, to select the new leader. This is an excellent example of the way Christians ought to seek the will of God in selecting leaders in the church. Verse 16 also gives a reason why a young person should seek the guidance of God in selecting a life companion. God knows both hearts, and He also knows all the future.

Verse 17, in the prayer of Moses, is a beautiful comparison of the people to a flock of sheep, and their shepherd to the leader whom God will choose. Moses here lets us know just how tenderly he cared for the people, in spite of their disobedience, and the way they so often tried his patience. This comparison of the people to a flock of sheep without a shepherd occurs again in I Kings 22:17; and is taken up by Jesus (Matt. 9:36; Mark 6:34).

Moses was told to ordain Joshua publicly so that the people would see Moses' attitude toward the new leader (v. 20). There was to be no hint of a power struggle or jealousy, but all must be done openly. It was in this act of passing on the leadership that Moses showed his true greatness. Many a great man has failed at this point by refusing to be gracious about letting a younger man take the place which he has filled so well. It takes a great man to lead, but a greater man to step down and help some other man lead.

Knowledge of the real meaning and nature of the Urim (v. 21) is almost completely lost in the past. Consultation of a good Bible dictionary will give a list of some of the theories, but little is definitely known. It is assumed that they were used in some way to learn the will of God in hard decisions.

E. Laws of Public Worship (28:1—29:40)

The purpose of this elaborate section is to give definite quantities for all the public sacrifices of the year, both the daily offerings, and the offerings on special days. As a result, it also presents a list of the annual religious festivals. Leviticus 23 also gives such a table of the religious festivals, but this section is unique in that it gives for each festival a specific date and a definite quantity for each sacrifice on that date. In the other books of the law there are scattered descriptions of such definite amounts, but the only other Old Testament list of specific amounts for all the special days and festivals is in Ezekiel 45:18—46:15. Yet the latter passage requires the prince to provide the offerings which are then offered in behalf of the people. So this passage is in some sense unique, and is supplementary to Leviticus 23.

The offerings here described are of four kinds: burnt offerings, meal offerings, drink offerings, and sin offerings. But nothing is new about these, as they are all found elsewhere. It is primarily the specific dates for the feasts and the specific amounts described for each which cause scholars of the last century to date this section in the exilic or post-exilic period. Wellhausen placed it after the time of Ezra, but many now feel that it could be as early as the Exile. There is a growing tendency to trace the Priestly material back to earlier times, at least in origin, if not in its present form. The fact is that it may not make a lot of difference whether this was written in its present form in the time of Moses or not. The theology of the passage is not affected by late dating, although the history of theology is affected.

The message of these two chapters is that God is interested in the way in which we worship Him. He is not to be approached lightly or casually. He is God, who made us and who is sustaining our lives and our universe at every moment. If we are to have a personal relationship with Him, it will be because He has graciously extended to us the invitation to come to Him, so He has the right to set the terms on which we will come.

The complicated appearance of the chapter may be cleared up by a chart.

Feast	Ref.	Date	Lambs	Rams	Bulls	Goats
Daily offerings	28:3-8	Each day	2			
Sabbath offerings	28:9-10	Each seventh day	2			
New Moon offering	28:11-15	First day of month	7	1	2	1
Passover	28:16		none listed			
Unleavened bread	28:17-25	Fifteenth to twenty-first days of first month (Each day)	7	1	2	1
Feast of Weeks	28:26-31		7	1	2	1
Feast of Trumpets	29:1-6	First day, seventh month	7	1	1	1
Day of Atonement	29:7-11	Tenth day of seventh month	7	1	1	1
Feast of Booths	29:12-38	Fifteenth to twenty-second days of seventh month				
Day 1			14	2	13	1
Day 2			14	2	12	1
Day 3			14	2	11	1
Day 4			14	2	10	1
Day 5			14	2	9	1
Day 6			14	2	8	1
Day 7			14	2	7	1
Day 8			7	1	1	1

Several points should be noted. Each animal offered required wine, oil, and meal to be offered also, as specified in 15:1-16. All animals are males and without blemish. Each special-day offering is in addition to whatever daily or sabbath offerings may be required for that day. The Passover is mentioned in 28:16, but no special offering is listed for that day; it was to be celebrated by families, rather than by public worship (cf. Exod. 12:1-25). These public offerings by the community were in addition to the individual offerings which were made from time to time.

These offerings served several purposes: they were an important part of the worship of the people; they furnishd food for the Levites and priests (cf. chap. 18); they symbolized the costliness of God's forgiveness of sinful man.

Jews have offered no sacrifices since the destruction of Herod's Temple in A.D. 70. Hebrews 9-10 makes clear that the death of Jesus is eternally effective for the removal of sin, and makes all animal sacrifices obsolete and unnecessary. That passage also makes clear that animal sacrifices were never effective in removing sin (Heb. 10:1-4), but that Jesus' death did effect this (10:5-14). Paul explains that the Christian, instead of offering animals, offers to God his own saved life as a sacrifice, pleasing God thereby (Rom. 12:1).

F. The Law on Women's Vows (30:1-16)

This section needs to be seen against the background of ancient Near Eastern culture, two aspects of which are important in this chapter. Written contracts and deeds were available, but for the average person oral vows were more common, so it was necessary for oral vows to be legally binding. Verse 3 therefore stresses the fact that an oral vow of any man must be kept (cf. Deut. 23:21 ff.; Eccl. 5:4-5; Matt. 5:33). The second aspect of ancient culture has to do with the place of women in society. Though the Old Testament does not consider women mere chattel, it does assume that they are subservient to men. The vows of most women were then subject to veto by the man responsible for each, and the conditions under which they were legally binding had to be specified. This is the only Old Testament passage dealing with the subject of women's vows.

It is *religious* vows which are discussed here, since the vows are "unto the Lord" (vv. 3-4). Two Hebrew words are used for vows in this chapter. *Nedher* is the broad term which can include all kinds of vows, but especially means positive vows to do something. *'Issar* is the vow of abstinence, promising to abstain from something, often for a limited time. In verse 13, where both words are used, the first is translated "vow" and the second "binding oath."

Three situations are considered, and rules laid down for them.

1. The vow of an unmarried woman living in her father's house, or a married woman living with her husband, is binding only if her father or husband does not object on the day he hears of the vow (vv. 3-8, 10-14). 2. The vow of a widow or a divorced woman is binding (v. 9). 3. If the husband of the married woman or the father of the unmarried woman does not annul the vow when he first hears of it, but later prevents her from keeping it, the sin is his, not hers (v. 15).

This chapter and the ruling in 27:1-11 were two steps taken

towards "women's liberation"! The basis for ultimate liberation is found in Galatians 3:28. So far as the relationship to Christ is concerned there can be no difference between male and female. The spiritual meaning of this is clear, but the exact social and cultural implications of the principle have to be hammered out over the centuries.

G. Extermination of the Midianites (31:1-54)

Moses was commanded to wage war against the Midianites (25:16-18) who had enticed the Israelites to idolatry, as was described so vividly in that chapter. That command is now carried out against those Midianites who lived in the vicinity of Moab. This was to be one of the last acts of Moses before his death (v. 2).

Without getting bogged down in some of the problems of this chapter, such as the large number of Midianites who were killed without the badly outnumbered Israelites losing a man, we can see the lessons this chapter teaches. 1. God is on the side of those who trust in Him, and gives victory over evil. 2. That which causes a person to fall into sin must be resisted to the end. 3. Even in war, the Israelites had to obey the religious commandments of cleansing from uncleanness. 4. War was to be so controlled that lust for booty did not prevail, and rules of dividing the spoil were to be followed.

1. The Expeditionary Force (31:1-6). First there is repeated the command to Moses to wage war against the Midianites (v. 2; cf. 25:17). Not all of the soldiers were to go out to the battle (v. 3a), since their purpose was not their own vengeance on enemies, but to uphold the honor and holiness of the Lord against the sin of Midian (v. 3b). Since this is the purpose, only a token army is sent, one thousand from each tribe, making a total of twelve thousand (vv. 4-5). For something of the same reason, they were led by Phinehas the priest (v. 6), who had taken such an active part in the original incident (25:6-8). The sacred trumpets (10:1-10) were taken along, and perhaps other objects from the sanctuary (though v. 6b may be calling the trumpets "sacred vessels"). All of these things show clearly that this was considered a holy war against the wicked enemies of God, and the idealized details with which the story is told all emphasize this fact.

Such a record as this, then, does not glorify war and fighting, but rather has the opposite effect. If God could not suddenly teach them to love their enemies (Matt. 5:43-48), He could at least teach them the first steps in bridling lust for war (cf. Deut. 9:1-6). We Christians notice also that the Old Testament makes no distinction between destroying evil and destroying the persons doing the evil. We know now that we must clearly make that distinction.

2. Defeat and Destruction of Midian (31:7-12). One of the problems of this passage is raised by the statement in verse 7 that they killed all the adult males of the Midianites. Yet we read in Judges 6 that Midian was a strong nation two centuries later. A solution often suggested is that this group comprised only a fraction of the Midianites, a colony who lived in the vicinity of Moab and Shittim.

Note that in addition to the five kings (leaders) who were killed, Balaam is also mentioned (v. 8). So we see that he did not get to "die the death of the righteous" as he had wished (23:10). The reason for this is given only in 31:16. How he came to be here in Midian at this time we can only speculate. The five leaders are also named in Joshua 13:21, but are called "princes" in that passage.

Verse 9 lists the captives and the spoils taken, and verses 11-12 tell that they brought all these back to the camp of the Israelites. Verse 10 tells of the burning of the cities and camps at Midian, so that the result was to bring the group involved to a virtual end.

3. Order to Exterminate Midian (31:13-18). The women and children had been brought back to camp. But this makes Moses angry, because, as he explains in verse 16, it was these very women who had enticed the Israelites into idolatry (25:1-2). He says here also that it was done at the instigation of Balaam; otherwise we have nothing recorded about his part in this. This verse 16 is the one to which reference is made in Micah 6:5; II Peter 2:15; Revelation 2:14. So Moses gives the order to kill all the women and children except the girl children, who can be kept for wives and slaves. This cruel order was not given as a general rule, but the nature of this occasion required it. The Canaanites as a whole were not exterminated, though some cities were.

From our perspective, more than three thousand years later, this was a cruel, heartless act. From their perspective, it was a religious act of high value to destroy those who had led them to sin against God. We must leave them to a merciful God, and live by all the light God has graciously let shine upon us.

4. Warriors' Purification (31:19-24). The point of this section is that even though the fighters were engaged in a religious act,

they had come into contact with the dead, and must be unclean for seven days (chap. 19). They must therefore obey all the rites for cleansing outlined in that chapter. As that chapter explained, this applied also to the booty which they had brought back with them. So all must go through the process of ritual cleansing.

5. Division of the Spoil (31:25-54). It is not important for us to memorize the details of this division of the booty of war. Yet the very fact that these details are specified can teach us something important about the attitude toward war. The soldiers who went into the battle were not going for the purpose of wreaking vengeance on enemies. They were going as representatives of the whole of the twelve tribes (vv. 3-6) to carry out the command of God (vv. 1-2). Since these soldiers represented the whole people of God, they could not selfishly keep for themselves all the booty they had taken. They had to share it equally with those who did not go out to fight (vv. 26-27). David later established this as a permanent rule of war (I Sam. 30:24-25).

Further, we are told that a religious tax had to be paid from the booty before it was distributed to individuals. First it was divided into two halves, one-half for the soldiers and one-half for the whole congregation. From the soldiers' half, five hundredths was given to the priests (vv. 28-29). From the congregation's part, one-fiftieth was given to the Levites (v. 30).

After a list of the total booty (vv. 32-46), we learn that the soldiers, in gratitude for the fact that God had protected them so that none were killed, gave a special thank offering of gold and jewelry (vv. 48-54).

H. Settlements in Trans-Jordan (32:1-42)

This section explains why two and one-half tribes settled east of the Jordan River. They were the tribes of Gad and Reuben, and the half-tribe of Manasseh.

1. Request of Gad and Reuben (32:1-5). So far, all the tribes had traveled and fought together. Now they were about ready to cross the Jordan River into Canaan proper. For the moment they were camped at Shittim, on the northern border of Moab (22:1). For some reason, the tribes of Gad and Reuben had more cattle than the other tribes (v. 1a) and were tired of driving them. They saw that the land they had all taken from Sihon (21:21-35) was excellent pasture land, so they asked to be allowed to settle there instead of crossing the Jordan (vv. 2-5).

2. Anger of Moses (32:6-15). Moses was disturbed at this request because it would divide the tribes. He felt that it was motivated by selfishness on the part of these tribes, who would settle down in territory won by all, while the other tribes went across and fought for land (v. 6).

He was also afraid that it would have the same effect as the majority report of the scouts thirty-eight years before (chaps. 13-14), and would discourage the people from entering into their land (vv. 7-15). This impassioned speech of Moses had just cause. He did not want to allow another mistake like the disastrous one at Kadesh, and would do anything in his power to prevent it (cf. Deut. 1:32-37; Ps. 95:8-11; Heb. 3:8-11).

3. Gad's and Reuben's Promises (32:16-19). The people of these two tribes, in response to Moses' fears, proposed to rebuild some of the captured cities into temporary places of safety for their cattle and families, while they themselves would cross the Jordan with the rest and help to subdue the land. They promised that they would not return to their own inheritance until each of the other tribes had secured their inheritances east of the Jordan (v. 19).

4. Moses' Permission (32:20-33). Moses agreed to this proposal, but warned the two tribes that if they did not keep their word, they would have to answer to God for it (v. 23). Since Moses knew that he would die before they crossed the Jordan, he strictly charged Eleazer the priest and Joshua, his successor, to see that the tribes kept their word (vv. 28-29).

Verse 33 tells us, with no previous preparation, that the half-tribe of Manasseh also took land east of the Jordan. So the two and one-half tribes took all the land which had been taken from Sihon and Og (21:21-35).

5. Cities Built by Gad and Reuben (32:34-38). What they actually did was to rebuild the destroyed cities enough to provide at least temporarily for their flocks and families. These names which included the names of idols were changed (v. 38).

6. Manassite Settlements in Gilead (32:39-42). According to 26:29-32, there were eight subsections of Manasseh, and six of them settled east of the Jordan. Other questions about this short section cannot be answered for lack of information.

VII. RECAPITULATION AND APPENDIXES (33:1–36:13)

A. Israel's Route from Egypt to Canaan (33:1-49)

This is one of the few sections which we are expressly told was written by the hand of Moses (v. 2). It serves as a summary of the whole journey of forty years from Egypt to the Jordan. If we omit the starting point in Egypt, and the final camp by the Jordan, there are forty camps listed. More than fifteen of them are not listed elsewhere in Scripture, and most of them cannot be definitely located, but that is not surprising. Tent dwellers do not leave the kind of remains that archeologists can use to make specific identifications.

With the names of the various campsites are given interesting allusions to events, some known and some totally unknown to us. Beyond that, this list is something like a family album, which is of great interest to the family, but can be somewhat boring to someone who does not know the persons in the pictures, and who does not therefore associate memories with each one.

B. Israel's Duty in Canaan (33:50-56)

Once more we are reminded that the people are encamped on the border of Moab, where they can look across the Jordan into the land which they are about to receive for their homeland. Their parents had been close long ago and had refused to enter in. We can imagine the thoughts which may have gone through the minds of these Israelites as they remembered that failure. Would they have the courage to succeed where their parents had failed?

At this point Moses breaks in on their thoughts with some instructions. He did not say to them, "If . . ." but "When ye are passed over . . . " (v. 51). He then reminds them of some of the things they must do when they get into Canaan (cf. Exod. 23:23-24).

The purpose of the instructions in this section is that they are to wipe out temptations to idolatry (cf. Exod. 34:11-17). Not only were the people to be driven out or put to death, but their places of pagan worship were to be destroyed (vv. 52-53). This was to be done for the sake of religious purity. The Canaanites were to be destroyed because of the wickedness of their religious practices, not because of hatred (Deut. 9:1-6).

Moses also instructed that the land was to be divided among the tribes by lot, to assure fairness (v. 54).

C. Tribal Boundaries in Canaan (34:1-29)

1. Boundaries Fixed (34:1-15). This section describes the ideal limits of the land of Canaan which God is about to give the Israelites for their possession. These ideal limits were achieved for only a short time during the reigns of David and Solomon. It was to be divided among the nine and one-half tribes which were to inherit west of the Jordan, since the tribes of Gad, Reuben, and half the tribe of Manasseh were settling east of the Jordan (v. 14; 32:33).

Many of the places marking the boundary are impossible to identify, especially on the northern border. It is enough to know that they were known at the right time. They are mentioned again in Joshua 15—19 and Ezekiel 47:13-20; 48:28.

2. Allotment Officers (34:16-29). In order to see that the division of the land was properly carried out, Moses named ten leaders of the people to oversee the process. He specifies that Eleazer the priest and Joshua will supervise the work of the ten. None of the princes of the tribes (Num. 1) when they left Egypt, nor their sons, is listed here. This was a new generation.

D. Levitical Cities (35:1-34)

1. Cities for the Levites (35:1-8). The Levites were not to inherit land of their own in the new land, but were to be given forty-eight cities in the other tribal allotments, with a portion of land attached to each. Joshua 21 tells how this was carried out.

The purpose of this seems to be two-fold: 1. It meant that the Levites, as religious leaders, would be scattered among the tribes where they could do the most good. 2. Since they were to be supported by tithes (18:23-24), it was appropriate and convenient for them to be located among the tribes in this manner.

2. Cities of Refuge (35:9-15). It was the custom in that day for the relatives of a murdered person to pursue the murderer and kill him in retribution for the crime. No doubt many innocent persons were killed in this way, as they are today in mob action. So Moses gave instruction which could help assure justice for suspected murderers.

Six of the Levitical cities (cf. vv 1-8) were to be set aside as "cities of refuge." They were to be places to which any accused murderer could flee for safety while his guilt was being determined. There were to be three of these on each side of the Jordan (v. 14).

Note that it was provided that such a one, like any other criminal or accused criminal, could be assured of a public trial (v. 12). This meant that there would be no lynching. The whole congregation had the right to see that justice was done.

3. Manslaughter and Murder (35:16-25). These verses are concerned with determining the conditions under which a person is guilty of murder, and when it is only unintentional manslaughter. The distinction seems to be that of motive. This concern for justice and the protection of the innocent is most commendable.

4. Legal Procedure and Warning (35:26-34). These rules lay down the legal procedure to be followed in the city of refuge. So long as the accused remains inside the city, he is safe. But if he leaves it, he may be put to death by the family of the murdered person. It required more than one witness to condemn a man (v. 30). No fine could be large enough to release the murderer, as it was too serious a crime (vv. 31-33).

It is not now understood why the death of the high priest should set the murderer free (v. 28).

E. Marriage of Heiresses (36:1-13)

This section is supplementary to 27:1-11, where it was decided that daughters could inherit property if there was no son. But now a situation is brought to light which could cause real complications in the tribal divisions of the land. The legal problem is presented to Moses and the leaders of the people for decision.

The problem situation is described in verses 3-4. If a woman has inherited property in the absence of sons, and then she marries a man from another tribe, her land would then belong to a man in a different tribe. This sort of thing could break down the whole division of the land among the tribes in a confusing manner.

The decision announced by Moses (vv. 6-9) is that any woman who owns an inheritance must not marry outside her own tribe. It is further explained that the daughters of Zelophehad (27:1-11), about whom the original problem had centered, did in fact marry according to this ruling (vv. 10-12).

Verse 13 apparently refers to all the commandments in Chapters 27–36.

APPENDIX

Ideas Related to Holiness

Five words related to holiness are used rather freely in the Pentateuch, but are not commonly understood. That is not surprising, since they come from a culture which is separated from us by half a world and by more than three thousand years. They also appear in Hebrew, a language which is quite different from English in its idioms. These particular words need a little fuller treatment than can be given in individual parts of the commentary, though this note does not presume to be comprehensive.

The words in Hebrew, with their common English translations, are: *Cherem* (devoted, or utterly destroyed), *qodesh* (holy), *chol* (common), *tame'* (unclean), and *tahor* (clean). These words are all related to the idea of holiness, but in ways that are not obvious. The problem is that the English words used for their translation do not give us the same connotations which the ancients had. It is an even deeper problem, because we do not even have these same concepts in our realms of thought. What we have to do to understand them is to try to feel our way into the culture of the ancient Near East so as to get some idea of the way they felt about certain things expressed by these words.

Let us begin with the word *qodesh*, usually translated "holy." To many English-speaking people the word *holy* signifies something sinless. Yet the basic meaning of *qodesh* is "wholly belonging to God, in a special relationship with God." This is seen in the fact that the opposite of *qodesh* is not "sinful," but "common" (*chol*)! Things which are common (*chol*) are not dedicated to God. They do not have a special relationship with God. They can be used for common, ordinary purposes. Persons who are holy have been wholly dedicated to the work of God. They belong to Him in some special sense. They have a special relationship with God, which sets them apart from all others and from all other ordinary purposes and work. There is a sense in which all the people of Israel were the people of God, and this is given repeatedly as the reason they must keep themselves from the customs and religions of the people around them. They were holy, and must refrain from all defilement. Other nations were common (*chol*), because they were not dedicated to God and did not have a personal relationship with Him.

The words *tame'* (unclean) and *tahor* (clean) are related to the first two as two parallel lines are related to each other. That is, *clean* does not mean "holy," and *unclean* does not mean "common." The thought is rather that that which is clean is capable of being made holy, and that which is unclean is incapable of being made holy. All persons could be made holy, but persons could be rendered temporarily unclean by a number of things, such as touching a dead person (Num. 5:1-2; 19:11 ff.). Such a person could not participate in the religious ceremonies until he had cleansed himself by the process outlined for such cleansing (Num. 19).

Some things were by nature thought of as unclean, and therefore unfit for any use by God in the Tabernacle. They were also unfit for human use and to be avoided. Swine, for example, were unclean.

A person could be unclean without being sinful. This is important to know when reading that touching a dead person, for instance, made one temporarily unclean. It was not a sin to touch one who had died, but simply rendered the person unclean for a season, and made it necessary for him to go through a cleansing ceremony, which included washing his body and his clothes. In the light of modern medical knowledge of transmissible diseases, that was a good rule! But the important aspect of this is that the uncleanness was ceremonial or religious. An unclean person or thing could not be dedicated to God until cleansed.

The remaining word is *cherem*, which is translated in a confusing variety of ways. One of the more common translations is "devoted." But it does not mean simply "devoted," but "devoted to some god other than the Lord God." This could be said of a thing or of a person. To be *cherem*, then, was far worse than to be "unclean." Some things which were *cherem* could be "undevoted" and then had to be dedicated to God. If they could not, then they had to be destroyed. If a person who was *cherem* because he served other gods chose to serve the Lord, then he had that right to dedicate himself to God and become holy to the Lord. If he did not so choose, he was to be destroyed. This is the reason the word is sometimes translated something like "utterly destroyed" (see Josh. 6:18). And this is the background for such commands as we find in Deuteronomy 20:10-18 and Joshua 6:17-19.

For further study of these words, see Norman H. Snaith *The Distinctive Ideas of the Old Testament*, New York; Schocken Books, 1964. Chapter 2.